"I Humbly Beg Your Speedy Answer"

"I HUMBLY BEG YOUR SPEEDY ANSWER"

Letters on Love & Marriage from the World's First Personal Advice Column

SELECTED, EDITED & INTRODUCED BY

MARY BETH NORTON

PRINCETON UNIVERSITY PRESS
PRINCETON & OXFORD

PUBLISHED BY PRINCETON UNIVERSITY PRESS
41 William Street, Princeton, New Jersey 08540
99 Banbury Road, Oxford OX2 6JX

press.princeton.edu

All Rights Reserved

ISBN 9780691253992
ISBN (e-book) 9780691254005

British Library Cataloging-in-Publication Data is available

EDITORIAL: Anne Savarese and James Collier
PRODUCTION EDITORIAL: Sara Lerner
TEXT AND JACKET DESIGN: Chris Ferrante
PRODUCTION: Erin Suydam
PUBLICITY: Alyssa Sanford and Carmen Jimenez
COPYEDITOR: Cathryn Slovensky

JACKET IMAGES: Details from *An Emblem of the Athenian Society* by Fredrik Hendrik van Hove. Frontispiece to *The Young Students Library* (1692), published by John Dunton. © The Trustees of the British Museum.

This book has been composed in IvyOra and Sweet Sans

PRINTED IN THE UNITED STATES OF AMERICA

1 3 5 7 9 10 8 6 4 2

This book is for my family—Clark, Catharine, Grael, Nona, Lia, and Mike—none of whom have ever written to a personal advice columnist (as far as I know)

CONTENTS

ACKNOWLEDGMENTS

I HAVE BEEN THINKING about preparing this edition for a long time, during which I described the project to many friends and colleagues. Recently, I asked some to read part or all of the manuscript, which they generously did, offering useful feedback. I thank Catherine Simpson Bueker (once my undergraduate research assistant and now a professor of sociology), Marty Farnsworth, Corinne Field, Julie Flavell, and Amy Silver Ritter, as well as my late partner, the marine biologist John B. Heiser, who did not live long enough to see the project come to fruition but who gave me wise counsel at its outset. I also thank the two anonymous readers for Princeton University Press for their helpful suggestions. Decades ago a then undergraduate research assistant, Jacqueline Kelly, transcribed some entries for me from the *Athenian Mercury* and the *Oracle*. (Today she is a New York City attorney, but still, I trust, interested in the Athenians.)

In addition, I thank my agent, George Lucas (and my friend Patrick Spero, who introduced me to George), and my Princeton University Press editor, Anne Savarese, both of whom made major contributions that helped turn an idea into a book. Sara Lerner shepherded the book through the production process, and Dimitri Karetnikov worked wonders with the illustrations, especially the London map. I appreciated the careful work of the copyeditor, Cathryn Slovensky, and Princeton University Press staff in general. At one point while I was working on this book, I was coping with a broken bone in my right foot. My good friend Gillian Sutherland took care of me for a crucial week, feeding me well while ensuring that I could keep the foot elevated to reduce the swelling.

An Emblem of ye Athenian Society. 1692.

London Printed For John Dunton at ye Rauen in ye Poultrey

John Dunton's "Question Project"

THE PUBLICATION THAT INITIATED the world's first personal advice column did not begin with that aim in mind. Rather, its founder, the printer John Dunton, envisioned a series of inexpensive single pages (broadsheets) printed on both sides, the eclectic contents of which would be supplied by questions from readers, with responses from Dunton and his associates. The successful venture—the *Athenian Gazette, or Casuistical Mercury*, known more succinctly as the *Athenian Mercury*—eventually published thousands of inquiries and replies on a wide variety of topics. But at the instigation of its readers, it also developed into a source of published advice on personal matters, the world's first. And it became the longest-lasting periodical in seventeenth-century England, its popularity at least partly a result of its public attention to private questions.

Dunton later recalled that he was walking in a London park with a friend one day in the early spring of 1691 when the idea for such a publication suddenly occurred to him. In retrospect, the premise seems simple, but in its own day it was unique. Dunton proposed a weekly broadsheet periodical aimed primarily at

FIGURE 1 (*opposite*). *An Emblem of the Athenian Society* by Fredrik Hendrik van Hove. Frontispiece to *The Young Students Library* (1692), published by John Dunton. This image presents the Athenian Society as a large group of bewigged experts responding to pleas from both wealthy querists (the top row) and ordinary folk (the lower row), with accompanying poetry. The first lines read "behind ye scenes sit mighty we / nor are we known nor will we be," indicating the initial anonymity of the Athenians. Collections of the Huntington Library, San Marino, California.

the male patrons of London's many coffeehouses. Those men, known for wide-ranging discussions held over the newfangled drink, would pose questions anonymously; the Athenian Society, supposedly a large team of experts but essentially comprising Dunton and his two brothers-in-law, Richard Sault and Samuel Wesley, would answer them.

Dunton, then thirty-two, was a bookseller with eclectic interests; Sault, his initial collaborator, was a part-time mathematical tutor; and the twenty-nine-year-old Wesley, whom they quickly recruited to join them, was a struggling clergyman and writer who probably welcomed the chance to earn extra income. Dunton, Sault, and Wesley drew up a formal contract for what Dunton called "the question project."

Sault and Wesley agreed to draft answers to questions Dunton supplied, to meet each week to go over them, and on Fridays to submit sufficient copy for the next week's issues. Dunton could then alter or reorder that copy as he wished. For their work, he promised to pay the two men together ten shillings a week after publication (the equivalent of approximately $140 in 2020 dollars). The broadsheets sold for a penny each to individual purchasers and by subscription to coffeehouses. Dunton at first concealed his involvement, identifying himself only as the Athenians' "bookseller." Letters were to be sent to a coffeehouse rather than to his print office, and Dunton did not publicly identify himself as the *Mercury*'s printer until many months had passed.

Dunton's project met with immediate success, developing into a major cultural phenomenon that spawned several rivals and even a parody in the form of a play, *The New Athenian Comedy*. The first call for questions on 17 March 1691 elicited such a plethora of queries that his initial plan quickly expanded to appearing twice weekly, on Tuesdays and Saturdays. Each broadsheet included eight to twelve questions and answers, or fifteen to twenty in a typical week. After twenty issues had appeared, Dunton bound the ephemeral one-page two-sided sheets into

Articles of agreem.t between Sam.ll Wesley Clerk Rich.d
Sault Gent. and John Dunton Stationer of London

Imprimis. That y.e s.d Wesley and Sault shall deliver into the hand of y.e s.d
s.d Dunton two distinct papers every Friday night each paper
to make halfe a printed sheet of the Athenian Gazett or mercury
which s.d paper is to be a performance of what is promis'd N.o 1: and N.o 7

Item. That y.e s.d Dunton shall have power to intermix and place
the said Questions as he pleases and shall pay 10 s Sterling for every
Number in print after N.o 4 the s.d mony to be adjusted once every
fortnight and the s.d mony not to be demanded before

Item. That the s.d Dunton shall be at liberty if he pleases to print
but one of the said papers every week which the s.d Sault is
to continue as he begun or the said Dunton is to be at
liberty to throw up the said paper when he pleases giving a
fortnights warening or paying upon demand 20 s Sterling a piece
to the s.d Wesley and Sault upon discontinuing the said papers

Item. That there be a meeting every Friday in the afternoon in
some convenient place betwixt the s.d Wesley and Sault to consult
of what they have done and to receive new Questions for the
next week and the party not coming before 3 of ye clock is
to forfeit one shilling to be spent and the party that has
not finisht his paper by that time excepting corrections shall
forfeit one shilling to be likewise spent

Item. That every volume which shall be N.o 30 shall have a preface and
Index to it the preface to be written by the s.d Wesley and Sault
for which they shall have 10 s betwixt em

Item. The said Wesley and Sault shall not desert the s.d undertaking
without giving the s.d Dunton a fortnights notice or paying
upon demand 20 s Sterling a piece for discontinuing the writing
of the said paper

Item. That the s.d Dunton shall not take any other person into
the s.d undertaking without the consent of the s.d Wesley
and Sault and y.t y.e s.d Wesley and Sault shall not engage
in the like undertaking for any other person but the s.d Dunton
upon the said Dunton performance of the above second Article

Item. That if the s.d Wesley or Sault should leave off the under=
=taking, the other shall be at liberty to engrosse the whole
or have equall power with the said Dunton in chuseing another
partner fitly qualified for the undertaking to continue the s.d paper
and that noe questions shall be put in that have not been seen
by the said Wesley and Sault

FIGURE 2. Contract of John Dunton, Richard Sault, and Samuel Wesley for what
would become the *Athenian Mercury*. 10 April 1691. The Bodleian Libraries, University of Oxford, MS. Rawl. D72, fol. 118r.

FIGURE 3. John Dunton published the *Athenian Mercury* from his print office "at [the sign of] the Raven in The Poultry," a short street in central London near other printers and coffeehouses. The dot marks its location. Heritage-Images / London Metropolitan Archives (City of London) / akg-images.

large volumes that his "Mercury women"—recruited from ubiquitous street vendors—hawked to coffeehouse owners for two shillings sixpence (about $35 in 2020 dollars), contending that customers would enjoy perusing them while chatting over hot beverages. The bound volumes contained indexes, allowing people to locate and read topics of interest in back issues, which in turn elicited more questions and helped to ensure the publication's continuation.

Eventually, Dunton produced twenty volumes, the last of which included only ten numbers (rather than the usual twenty, plus frequent supplements), because the final period of publication included a months-long hiatus that followed the death of his wife. A few years later, beset by financial difficulties, he sold the copyright to another printer, Andrew Bell, who produced a three-volume compilation titled *The Athenian Oracle*. In that version, the *Mercury*'s contents remained available to readers even into the nineteenth century.

The questions, which Dunton anticipated as a coffeehouse habitué himself, ranged widely over many subjects. Among the inquiries were some on the Bible (Who was Cain's wife? Did Adam and Eve eat actual apples?), science (What is a star? Why

To be plain, we are senfible 'tis in your Power to Damn or Save a poor Paper at your Pleafure, let Bookfeller or Author do what they will : You are the Meffengers of Fate, and a Bloody Fight it felf won't do without your Pains and Labour —— So much for Interest, now a little for Gratitude —— We muft own Athens had fallen long e're this, had not you (like Minerva's as you are) ftrennuoufly fupported it ; not Vander's felf e're Walkt more dirty Steps than you on its behalf, nor with more Vigour declaims againft its Rivals and Enemies—— And befides all this, there's fomething of Kindred in the Cafe, at leaft we are half Name-fakes, a quarter of which wou'd be more than fufficient whereon to ground a Dedication. Thus wifhing you good Cuftomers to your New Votes of Parliament, and brave roaring News twice a Week for this Seven Years next enfuing, We reft,

And all that.

FIGURE 4. Portion of the preface to volume II of the *Athenian Mercury* (11 July–21 October 1693), dedicated to "the Worshipfull Society of Mercury Women," who sold newspapers and broadsheets to the London public and were "half Namesakes" to the publication itself. Without them, Dunton wrote, his venture would have failed. Division of Rare and Manuscript Collections, Cornell University Library.

does a dolphin follow a ship until frightened away?), medicine (What causes smallpox? Can a crooked person be made straight again?), military tactics (Is it better to attack an enemy's country or to guard one's own?), and law (If a man dies, does his apprentice have to serve the widow?). The three men occasionally consulted others for expert opinions, but their contract forbade additions to the team, and no one else ever formally joined their enterprise or participated more than sporadically. Dunton had created a source where coffeehouse patrons could find answers to questions that arose in their discussions or ask additional ones not previously dealt with in the *Mercury*.

The Athenians tried to eschew politics, since the topic was especially fraught after a dramatic change of government two years earlier. In 1689, Protestant members of Parliament had ousted the Catholic Stuarts from the English throne, formally concluding decades of turmoil that had begun in the 1640s with civil war between Parliament and the Stuart monarchs. The Protestant Mary II and her Dutch cousin and husband, William of Orange, jointly assumed the throne in 1689, but their rule was still contested by many supporters of the Stuarts. Even after 1695, when Parliament's 1643 censorship law for "correcting and regulating all abuses of the press" was allowed to lapse, Dunton tried to avoid including political opinions in the *Mercury*, other than broadly supporting the regime of William and Mary. A several-month suspension of publication during 1692, caused by a communication that ran afoul of the censors, taught Dunton an important lesson that stayed with him for the rest of the decade.

After just a few weeks, the publication's anonymous correspondents began to broach a theme that the three men had not anticipated: inquiries about personal relationships, including courtship, marriage, and sexual behavior. The first set of such questions—thirteen in all—came from a man; the Athenians printed them and their answers in the thirteenth issue in early May 1691. Those queries were broadly and impersonally phrased: for example, Should a person marry someone they "cannot" love in order to gain access to a good estate? Don't most people marry too young? Is a woman worse off in marriage than a man?

In the same issue, the Athenians noted another unexpected development: "a lady in the country" had written to inquire "whether her sex might not send us questions as well as men." Dunton's initial publication plan centered on an exclusively male audience, for only men frequented coffeehouses, although some women worked in them. That letter surely surprised Dunton and his colleagues, not only because it came from "the country" instead of London but also because it was from a woman, who must have accessed the *Mercury* through a male relative or acquaintance. Yet the Athenians adapted quickly, explaining that they would "answer all manner of questions sent to us by either sex." Accordingly, a few weeks later a woman submitted a similar group of impersonally phrased questions (e.g., Is it proper for women to be learned? Is beauty real or imaginary?), which the Athenians answered in their eighteenth issue in late May 1691. The next month, at the end of what became the first bound volume, they responded to the first explicitly personal query they received—from a man accused of fathering a child out of wedlock (included in the selections in this book, along with several other examples of the initial questions). And so, when Dunton gathered the broadsheets to create the second volume, he changed the title page to reflect openness to female as well as male querists, as he termed those submitting questions.

Without intending to do so, and wholly in response to queries posed by their readers, the Athenians had initiated the first personal advice column ever published. Anonymity was clearly the key: concealing the identity of correspondents formed a part of Dunton's conception of "the question project" from the outset. A survey of a randomly selected volume (six, published in early 1692) by the scholar Helen Berry revealed that nearly one-third of the more than two hundred inquiries in that volume fell into the category of questions about personal relationships. Dunton often grouped such queries from both men and women into "ladies issues"; in the first five volumes, 45 percent of those inquiries came from men and 23 percent from women; 33 percent were not identifiable by gender.

Although the Oxford-educated Wesley was the only formally trained cleric in the group, Dunton was the son and grandson of ministers, and the three men shared a broadly based Protestant outlook. They aligned themselves with the campaign for the Reformation of Manners, a movement led by Queen Mary II that sought to combat perceived excesses of the day, especially prostitution and clandestine marriage. Themes of religion, sexuality, and morality were entwined in the minds of both the *Mercury*'s readers and the Athenians themselves. Their responses to correspondents who described various types of sexual misbehavior rarely expressed sympathy for questioners' plight but instead frequently decried the immorality involved. Yet occasionally even in such instances the advice offered was judicious and must have been welcome.

FIGURE 5. *The Coffeehouse Mob*, frontispiece to part 4 of *Vulgus Britannicus: or the British Hudibras* by Edward Ward (London, 1710). The male patrons read newspapers and broadsheets like the *Athenian Mercury* while they argue, drink, and smoke. In the rear, a female employee—the only woman in the room—serves coffee; next to her, coffeepots heat on a large stove. Collections of the Huntington Library, San Marino, California.

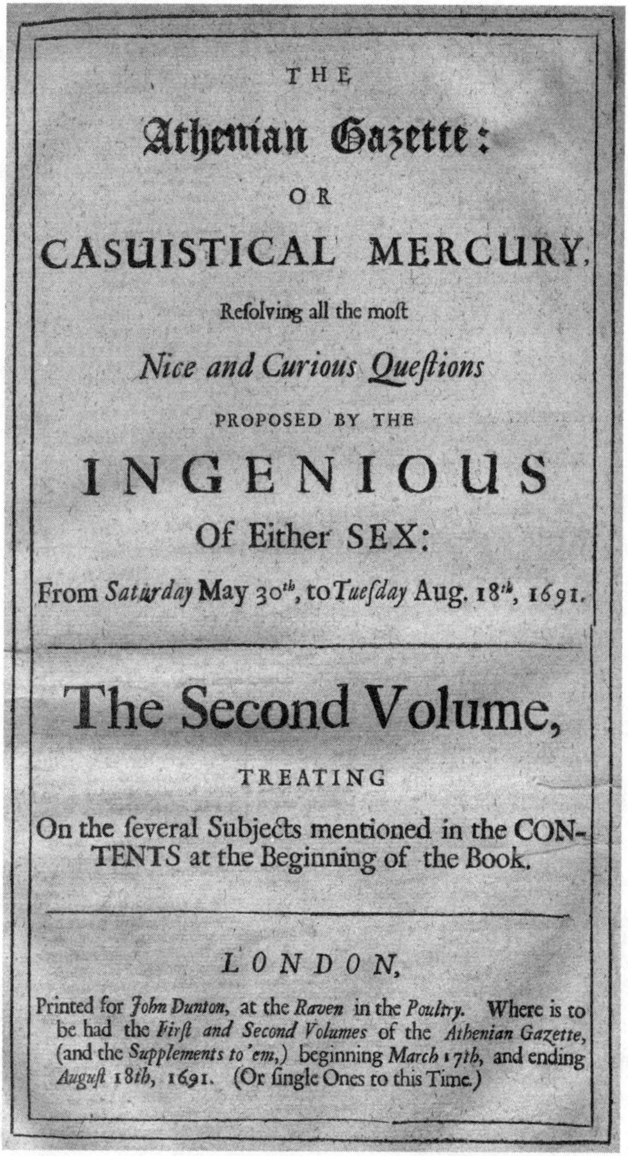

THE

Athenian Gazette:

OR

CASUISTICAL MERCURY,

Refolving all the moft

Nice and Curious Queftions

PROPOSED BY THE

INGENIOUS

Of Either SEX:

From *Saturday* May 30*th*, to *Tuefday* Aug. 18*th*, 1691.

The Second Volume,

TREATING

On the feveral Subjects mentioned in the CON-
TENTS at the Beginning of the Book.

L O N D O N,

Printed for *John Dunton,* at the *Raven* in the *Poultry.* Where is to
be had the *Firft* and *Second Volumes* of the *Athenian Gazette,*
(and the *Supplements to 'em,*) beginning *March* 17*th,* and ending
Auguft 18*th,* 1691. (Or fingle Ones to this Time.)

FIGURE 6. The second bound volume of the *Athenian Mercury* added the line
"of either sex" to the title page, which reflected the Athenians' openness to receiving questions from men and women alike. Division of Rare and Manuscript
Collections, Cornell University Library.

One anonymous reader, after perusing broadsheets that contained what they termed "pitiful" personal inquiries, charged the Athenians with detracting from the publication's learned reputation by dealing with such matters. But Dunton and his colleagues insisted on the importance of the topics their correspondents raised. "Many questions not only have an influence on the happiness of particular men and the peace of families, but even the good and welfare of larger societies and the whole commonwealth, which consists of families and single persons," the Athenians commented [3:13, 8 September 1691].[1] So, ignoring the pointed criticism from at least one member of their audience, the Athenians continued to offer personal advice to those who asked for it. And many continued to ask... for the next six years.

The questions, whether accurately representing the correspondents' own experiences or not (some said they were writing on behalf of "a friend," which the Athenians often explicitly recognized as a fiction), open a remarkable window into the private lives of men and women in an era long before our own. Even though the queries often formally referred to the problems of "gentlemen" and "ladies," their content reveals that the authors were not for the most part drawn from the ranks of the very wealthy but instead had middling status or aspired to upward mobility. Many, though by no means all, were young, just starting out in marriage or a trade. They confronted all the problems common to that stage of life, including conducting courtships, acquiring property, and engaging in premarital negotiations. In an era in which literacy was increasing significantly, especially in the ranks of urban tradesmen and tradeswomen, reading and writing were no longer optional but required skills for those who hoped to improve their lot in life.

---

1 See the last paragraph in this introduction for an explanation of citation practice.

Many specific circumstances differ from those in the twenty-first century. Custom and law dictated that young people should defer to their parents when deciding whom to marry. If parents refused consent, the Athenians might suggest that youthful questioners should not marry at all, or should postpone a wedding until after they reached the age of twenty-one or their parents had died. Yet at times they also could offer helpful advice on how to persuade recalcitrant parents to accept a son's or daughter's choice of a spouse. Financial prospects were thought to be nearly as important to successful marriage formation as love or affection, so money frequently played a role in questions and answers about wedlock, especially when parents were involved. (Yet the Athenians usually stressed the importance of love, or at least affection, over finances.) Within the bonds of matrimony, Athenians and others expected husbands to take the lead in all marital affairs, but exceptions were possible.

Perhaps most striking in many letters is the evident confusion about what constituted a valid marriage. Parliament did not adopt a marriage law until 1753, and so six decades earlier a person's matrimonial status could appear uncertain. The Church of England placed great emphasis on the mutual consent of couples as embodied in explicit promises of marriage and premarital contracts. Canon law after 1604 nominally insisted that people be married by a clergyman in a church, but requirements for place and time were so restrictive that in practice they were often circumvented. Correspondents wondered about what constituted enforceable marriage contracts and whether or how they could be voided. Indeed, writers sometimes expressed uncertainty about whether they were married or to whom, with several identifying multiple possible spouses. Confronted by their readers' confusion, the Athenians offered varying definitions of their own, usually insisting that public ceremonies in church were important, but at other times stressing that mutual consent in private was the key to a valid marital union.

Adding to the uncertainties surrounding marriage, under ecclesiastical law formal divorces were almost impossible to obtain, thus encouraging informal solutions to problems posed by marital difficulties. The Athenians' advice to those complaining of abusive spouses—especially offered to mistreated wives—tended to be limited to a few unappealing options, such as turning to charity from the church for assistance for oneself and children. One man termed the quest for divorce "tedious" when he explained why he simply exchanged one wife for another without attempting to follow legal procedures. Even if an ecclesiastical court allowed a divorce "from bed and board" (essentially, a separation agreement obtainable on proof that a partner had committed adultery), neither partner could legally remarry as long as the other lived. Correspondents themselves proposed or adopted a variety of creative solutions to the divorce conundrum, most of them illegal and immoral in the Athenians' eyes.

Although marriage laws are less confusing in the twenty-first century, other dilemmas described in the *Mercury* still appear frequently in newspaper and magazine advice columns. Lonely people wondered how best to meet and attract a potential partner. Some correspondents sought methods to ease a conscience troubled by prior misbehavior. Spouses asked how to handle contentious marriages while remaining wedded to each other. Writers complained about tense relationships with in-laws. Both men and women disclosed entering into intimate relationships they later regretted, inquiring about how to extract themselves with the least amount of difficulty. When one half of a courting couple began "slighting"—in modern parlance, "ghosting"—the other, the injured party would request guidance. And many single or married people admitted to engaging in sex outside of wedlock, detailing subsequent emotional and financial tangles with complex implications they asked the Athenians to address.

The Athenians were men of their own time but were also more supportive of women—and thus less misogynistic—than most, and they prided themselves on that attitude. Through their openness to queries posed by women, and responses that stressed the same standards of sexual probity for both male and female correspondents, they underscored their relatively evenhanded treatment of gender politics. Yet simultaneously they expressed attitudes toward lower-status individuals and children that today's readers will likely find jarring.

I first encountered the contents of the 1690s letters while researching an earlier book, *Separated by Their Sex: Women in Public and Private in the Colonial Atlantic World* (published in 2011). Since I am a scholar of women's and gender history, the similarities and differences of the personal concerns of today and those of more than three centuries ago attracted my interest. Contemporary advice columns by authors like Amy Dickinson and Carolyn Hax follow in the footsteps not only of early twentieth-century columnists like "Beatrice Fairfax" (Marie Manning Gasch), of the Hearst syndicate, and mid-twentieth-century columns by "Ann Landers" and "Dear Abby," but also of the Athenians. Unlike such modern writers, Dunton and his colleagues had not intended to become "agony aunts" but followed the lead of their readers in doing so. In that regard the correspondents of the *Athenian Mercury* resembled the Jewish immigrants who, in 1906, began to write anonymously in Yiddish to the editors of *Der Forverts* (*The Forward*) to request advice, leading to the publication of a regular column, *A Bintel Brief*.

I selected the questions and answers that follow from the twenty volumes of the *Athenian Mercury* and the subsequent compilation, *The Athenian Oracle*, with the aim of revealing the sort of personal problems for which readers in the late seventeenth century sought advice from the Athenians. As a reputed large group of experts, the three men responded to wide-ranging inquiries with an aura of authority that persisted even after Dunton's key role became known.

Although I have chosen to focus solely on queries about courtship, marriage, and sexual behavior, some questions to the Athenians raised other practical or ethical issues (e.g., Should a witness expose a thief? Where can a man who has spent his inheritance find honest employment?). The letters illuminate themes common in the 1690s in their emphasis on the interconnections among religion, morality, law, and sexuality. Did the writers truthfully describe their circumstances or possibly those of actual acquaintances? Even in the 1690s readers occasionally charged the Athenians with making it all up, but Dunton and his associates insisted that they faithfully recorded the questions they were asked, and sometimes they, too, wondered in print if the letters might be fictional. They do appear to have edited more than a few queries for grammar and clarity.

Accordingly, it is perhaps appropriate that as editor I have done the same. Seventeenth-century prose is often convoluted, with phrasing, capitalization, punctuation, and spelling alien to current readers. I have shortened sentences and modernized and regularized the language of both correspondents and Athenians. Ellipses indicate places where I have cut extraneous phrases for ease of reading, except when lengthy sentences precede or follow the passages I have edited, when ellipses are omitted. I have also rephrased or summarized convoluted sentences replete with double negatives to make them easier to understand, and I have silently replaced words unknown today or those whose meaning has changed since the 1690s. Despite these editorial alterations, I have sought to retain as much of the original language and phrasing as possible so that readers can see the individuality of the correspondents and the Athenians' various replies. One word I have not changed is "spark," which they used in a deprecating manner to refer to problematic beaus courting young women. Another I have not altered is "friends," which seventeenth-century writers used to refer to parents or, more broadly, relatives in general, a usage that becomes evident in many of the questions and answers.

Vol. 3.   **Numb. 13.**

The Athenian Mercury:

Tuesday, September 8. 1691.

Quest. 1. *How may a Man reclaim a head-strong or unruly Wife?*

Answ. Give her Rope enough — Our meaning is, e'ne let her alone, for she's not to be made Civil by any thing but the Worms. But if you have a mind to try what Hand you have at *working Miracles*, you may make use of some of these following Directions: *Watch her Tyms* — that's the *last Remedy first*; this is a way to tame even Lyons, and it may Tygers too: Some have gotten a *Dram*, and beat it so long 'till their poor Women have been struck perfectly Dumb and Deaf with the Noise on't. Some are for *Letting her Blood* — if any where, 'twou'd be best one wou'd think *under the Tongue*, or in both Arms, to prevent her Scolding or Fighting. Others are for *Drawing her Teeth*, which wou'd do well enough if they cou'd Cut the Nails tooat the same time : But the surest way of all is, being a *good Husband your self*, for 'tis bad Husbands are very often the Cause that the Wives are no better than they shou'd be.

Quest. 2. *Is't probable there will be any Sexes in Heaven?*

Answ. We believe not — Our Saviour says, that *there they neither Marry nor are given in Marriage*: and if so, what *Need of Sexes?* and why that in Heaven which there's *no Need of?* All that's of the Essence of a Man will undoubtedly be there, and that's a rational Soul united to an *organiz'd Body*; but what Organs will be necessary then we can't tell, however these cannot. Besides, this difference is only accidental, *Man and Woman being the Essence the same*. But in a State of Bliss and Perfection, all that's Imperfect or Accidental shall be removed, and accordingly one wou'd think *Sexes shou'd*. We won't add for another Reason what, as we remember, one of the Fathers has said — That *were there any Woman in Heaven, the Angels cou'd not stand long*, but wou'd certainly be seduced from their Innocency, and Fall as *Adam* did.

Quest. 3. *Two Friends see the same Lady in the same day, the first bringing the second to see her, asking his Advice, and desiring his assistance in the Amour — He on his seeing her, falls also desperately in Love with her — Whether of the two in this Case ought to desist? and whether if both Address, their Friendship is not thereby actually dissolv'd and ruin'd?*

Answ. 'Twou'd be generous if in this Nice Case he that saw her last wou'd for that Reason give up all to his Friend, — 'twou'd be more *prudent* if both cou'd prevail upon themselves to quit their Enterprize — But 'tis not very proper to talk either of *Generosity* or *Prudence* in Love. To give our Sence freely, we believe it next to *impossible their Friendship shou'd be long-liv'd* ; but the only way to make 'em so, is for both to continue their Addresses fairly and handsomly, without any Reflections or Derogation by one of the other, to leave the Decision to the Lady her self or Lady Fortune ; and for him that has her — *Happy Man be his Dole?*

Quest. 4. *Whether it does not weaken the Credit of the Athenian Mercury, that the Authors of it descend to such a pitiful Employment as to take Notice of Feminine Impertinencies?*

Answ. Now dare we venture a good Wager, tho' that way of Trading is now a little out of Fashion, that the Querist is *stout sour, old, surly, or young, disappointed Lover* ; or else a grave Philosophical Don, so *perfectly refin'd*, that he's made up of nothing but Spirit and Notion : But leaving Guesses, we must tell him we are troubled with Ten, perhaps a Hundred *Masculine Impertinencies* to one Feminine, as he himself wou'd find, if he was for some *half Hour to read our Letters*. Whereas, on the other side, we have Letters upon the File from Ladies, and those without the *loathed Advantages of Learning*, which are of so great Concern, and carry so much weight, that we dare not without considerable *Time* and *Thought* attempt their Answer. For medling with Questions of *Courtship, Love* and *Marriage*, we might say we design'd thereby to mingle the *Dulce* and the *Utile*, that one might

like a gilded Pill or sweeten'd Potion get down the other. But we scorn to Excuse what needs it not, but rather ought to be glory'd in, since tho' some things of this Nature may be *pure Matters of Gallantry*, yet there are very many Questions which not only have an Influence on the Happiness of particular Men, and the *Peace of Families*, but even the good and welfare of larger Societies, and the whole Commonwealth, which consists of Families and single Persons ; the Instances whereof need not be more distinctly remarkt to the Observing Reader.

Quest. 5. *Whether our Laws against Adultery, and the Proof of it, ben't too favourable to the Women? and whether this be not an Encouragement to Offenders?*

Answ. If those Laws, and the Proof required, be too favourable to the *Women*, they are so to the *Men* also, there being *no essential Evil* in the Crime committed by one, which is not in the others. And tho' next to Impunity in this Case may render the Persons concerned more confident and impenitent than they would otherwise be, and perhaps than the *good of Society* requires, yet if they cou'd last look on a little further into the other World, they'd find Punishment sufficient to deterr 'em from that and all other such hainous Offences.

Quest. 6. *Will Love and Friendship continue after this Life?*

Answ. To us it seems probable they may — as *whatever is rational* and seems to depend on the Mind, not the Body. 'Tis probable that there's such a thing as *Friendship among Angels*, for Love each other undoubtedly they must, and love more intensely they may, since as have the most *beautiful Characters of the Divine Power and Goodness* upon them : Now we shall be like the Angels, and may therefore have Friendships as well as they.

Quest. 7. *Which is the stronger, Friendship or Love?*

Answ. Love ; for it snaps asunder the strongest and best-laid Friendships in the World in the *Case of Rivals*, and totally sucks it up and drowns it, where between different Sexes, and Love succeeds in its room.

Quest. 8. *Is there any real force in Charms, Amulets, Love-powder, Potions, &c. to procure Love?*

Answ. For Charms, if there's any thing in 'em, *abstracted from Fancy*, as we have already discours'd, it must be Diabolical — but they can't do no more than the Devil himself, who can only *represent the Object*, not force the Will to embrace it : All your *Rabble of Amulets, Talismans, &c.* we look upon to be of the same Nature, and their Planetary Influences perfectly unaccountable, if not ridiculous. *Love-powder* and *Potions* there may be with a Vengeance, but then they are all Natural, and rather *move Desire than Love*, *and may command the Body, but never touch the mind*. The only lawful Philtre or Charm then to procure Love, is Love, attended with Zeal, Assiduity, and Discretion, and *illustrated with fair and virtuous Actions*.

Quest. 9. *Why Women are generally fondest of Men that are most regardless of 'em? — and since they are so, if she'll have reason to complain for the future if all Men shou'd slight 'em?*

Answ. To the first — if taken generally, as there exprest, 'tis the farthest thing in the World from being true : *'Tis Love is the Cause of Love*, and it must be a strange sort of an Antiperistasis indeed if Scorn shou'd produce it, since the Effect wou'd then contrary to the Axiom, be absolutely different from the Cause whence 'twas deriv'd. It's true, there may be some little Coquets of this Humour, who may be troubled with the same Caprice that *Hudibras's* Mistress was, who plainly tells her, *Poor despairing Lover — I cannot love if I'm belov'd* — But it's impossible any Woman of sense or generosity can be guilty of so mean a Folly ; though some may perhaps out of a *Pique of Modesty*, to comply with Custom, or to make the Lover more eager, at first refuse what they Love, and having tired 'em out, repent too late their

The book is organized into six topical chapters: courtship, choosing a spouse, parental consent, promises and vows, matrimony, and dangerous liaisons. On occasion the themes in the different sections overlap; readers should not expect neat divisions.

Citations accompany every question-and-answer pair, so readers who wish to do so may consult the originals in the digital ProQuest British Periodicals Collection; in the Burney Collection at the British Library (available digitally through Gale Primary Sources); or in surviving published copies of the *Mercury* or the *Oracle*. I was fortunate to have access to such printed copies at the Cambridge University Library, the Huntington Library, and the Cornell University Library at various times during my research, as well as to the online sources, thanks to Cornell University's subscriptions to the online services.

The citations, in square brackets after each Q & A, take the following form: the correct question number (preceded by Q and occasionally followed by another number, in curly brackets, when the printed number was incorrect); the volume number; the issue number, when there is one; and the publication date, when given. Sometimes, especially when the Q & A is from a supplement printed at the end of a volume, there are missing dates or issue numbers, which are identified to the extent possible.

CHAPTER 1

"Kissing Is a Luscious Diet"

COURTSHIP

GENERAL QUESTIONS ABOUT COURTSHIP appeared among the first set of personal inquiries published in the *Mercury* in May 1691. Although some writers persisted in asking such general queries, later correspondents were more likely to describe specific circumstances they wanted the purported experts to address. Because the *Mercury* had many youthful readers, such questions composed a significant proportion of personal queries posed to the Athenians. Both men and women wondered about the best ways to deal with the opposite sex and how to achieve the desired end of engagement to an appropriate partner.

Women and men commonly had different concerns. Women, for example, hoped to preserve their modesty while still conveying interest in men's advances, whereas men requested advice about dealing with rival suitors or asked the Athenians to interpret what they saw as inexplicable behavior by the women they were courting. Both concurred in wondering about possible limits to appropriate courting behavior, and women in particular were concerned about how to handle men who had breached the rules. Both, too, described their anguish at being "slighted" by the person they loved.

Q. *Is it permissible to make addresses to young ladies without a prior acquainting their parents and relatives therewith?*

A.   A general conversation with a lady is requisite to know (if possible) whether she deserves to be loved, and this before any application be made to the parents for liberty for a formal courtship. Were I a lover, I should choose to make an approach to young and old at nearly the same time so that neither might conceive any umbrage of each other.... There is also a great difference between immediate parents and more remote relations and perhaps, too, between some parents and others. [Q.1, 1:13, 5 May 1691]

Q.   *Is a public or private courtship best?*

A.   A private is the more safe as well as the more pleasant.... Every assignation in a secret amour has infinitely more gusto and relish in it than a formal public interview on purpose for two persons to talk fine things and look sillily upon one another.... Nor has a private amour less advantage to the safety than the pleasure of it, especially where there are rivals.... Whether it is more honorable or no, none but those concerned can resolve. [Q.3, 1:13, 5 May 1691]

Q.   *What course must a person take to remove a lady's aversion to him?*

A.   Be so often with her that she can dream of nothing but you. This only recipe has the greatest effect on most of the fair sex, who if you hold on long enough will be forced at last to love you in their own defense. [Q.4, 1:13, 5 May 1691]

Q.   *How shall a man know when a lady loves him?*

A.   First find out, if you can, whether she has ever loved any other before, for that renders the case much more difficult, for one that has been deceived herself knows how to deceive you. Jealousy is counted one pretty sure sign of love.... If a woman tells you she loves you, there's no way but believing her. Few of the tokens of that passion are infallible, though the surest sign that a woman loves you is her marrying you. [Q.14, 1:13, 5 May 1691]

Q. *Is absence or presence best for love?*

A. The latter in the beginning of an amour, the former when it's confirmed and already settled. It is dangerous at first, because it gives a rival opportunity to make addresses.... But where the main dispute is once over and the heart fairly won, the case is much altered. Then perhaps being always present is one of the most dangerous, though desired, things that can befall a lover.... Faults will daily be found, unlucky accidents will fall out, such things will be revealed as would never have been suspected nor believed, a thousand little quarrels and piques will arise, which at least produce vexation, oftentimes a final parting. But now in absence the quite contrary happens. We willingly forget the faults of those we love and magnify their excellencies. We embrace and cherish their dear ideas and memories.... And if we hear, especially by letters, our love is extremely increased by those little subtle messengers.... When the lovers come once to meet again, there's such ado with transports, raptures, and the rest, that, in a word, we dare think no longer on it. [Q.6, 2:13, 7 July 1691]

Q. *Is there any real force in charms, amulets, love-powder, potions, etc., to procure love?*

A. The only appropriate...charm to procure love is love, combined with zeal, assiduity, and discretion, and illustrated with fair and virtuous actions. [Q.8, 3:13, 8 September 1691]

Q. *I see in some of your former* Mercurys *that you blame the female sex for being too credulous and wonder why we aren't more careful about whom we believe. Pray be so kind to teach us your skill. When a man courts us, how shall we know whether it's for marriage or for diversion, or any other reason?*

A. So difficult a question that we believe many a man can scarce resolve it himself in the time of his courtship. Like other common swearers and liars, he might have told his tale so often that he believes it himself. . . . There are indeed so many equivocations in love that it's much easier to be in the wrong than in the right. . . . We must therefore return to our old infallible rule. If a man does really marry you, you may believe he courted you for marriage at least, if not for love, but woe be to you if you believe him upon his word and honor, faith, and conscience. A parcel of strong words in the matrimonial service will have and hold him to the grindstone when all the other lies are as easily broken as made. Then it's ten to one that he forsakes you, laughs at you, and exposes you into the bargain. [Q3, 17:4, 13 April 1695]

Q. *How may a true lover be distinguished from a false one?*

A. A man who loves sincerely will not only be careful not to omit anything that can be of any real service to his mistress, but he'll also be very assiduous to do everything which he thinks can please her. The false one may endeavor to counterfeit in the same way, yet those acts will be merely artifice and not a pure effect of love. So if he's observed for some time, a curious eye will at some moments perceive less ardor. [Q7, 18:14, 31 August 1695]

The Athenians replied seriously to two women who asked where they could most easily find husbands, but when they were asked to help a man find a wife, they treated the letter as a joke, which it undoubtedly was. (Some single Englishwomen in the seventeenth century are known to have done what the Athenians advised.)

Q. *What is the likeliest place to get a husband in?*

A. Poor distressed lady! Had we but her name, we should . . . insert an advertisement for her at the end of our *Mercury.* But since she has left us in the dark, she must be content with the best directions we can give her. . . . We answer then that the likeliest place to get a lover is where there are fewest women. Accordingly, if she will venture to ship herself to the colonies by the next fleet . . . ten to one but one or other there will fulfill her wish. [Q.5, 2:13, 7 July 1691]

Q. *A young woman growing into years wishes to know what she shall do to get her a good husband?*
A. We answer briefly: go to the colonies, or send her name to us, nor can we think of any other remedy. [Q.4, 13:19, 10 April 1694]

Q. *I have an earnest request to you on behalf of a young gentleman. He has a very good estate in money, is well built, has a very comely face, and an excellent head of hair. This agreeable person desires you would oblige him by helping him to find a wife equal to him in those respects.*
A. We believe his character is too well known to succeed in this search among his regular acquaintances, or else he'd never address such a request to strangers. But perhaps a woman might be in similar circumstances. Therefore, being charitable, we are willing to bring the fools together, and in order to do that we think each of them should publish their names either in the *Gazette* or by a common crier. [Q.3, 16:11, 22 January 1695]

Women's questions about courtship behavior tended to focus on their attempt to maintain a modest demeanor.

Q. *When we are in love and the men won't or can't understand our signs and motions, what in modesty can we do more to open their eyes?*
A. Alas, poor lady! Your case is very hard. Why, pull them by the nose, write to them, or if neither of these will do, . . . show them this question and answer in the *Athenian Mercury*. [Q.20, 3:4, 8 August 1691]

Q. *If a lady is in love with a man, is it permissible for her to ask his consent?*

A. Yes, yes, poor creature, it's hard to starve out of politeness, failing to ask for meat when we are hungry. [Q.6, 6:7, 23 February 1692]

Q. *A lady who is in love desires to know how she may decently convince the other person of her passion?*

A. Indeed, Madam, it's a ticklish point, and you should know a man well before you try anything. . . . To be plain with you, we find men to be an ungrateful sort of an animal in such cases. . . . But the best way will be to do it as decently as you can. First try to lead him into knowing how you feel. If that does not work, write to him. Then if that fails, tell him frankly about it, and so accustom him to your feelings that he may be forced to love you in his own defense. But be well assured of his attitude before you venture on to marriage. [Q.7, 14:7, 12 June 1694]

Q. *I desire your opinion in this question: May a woman in love make it known without any breach of modesty? Nay, would she not rather be commended for speaking her mind than to be silent like a fool?*

A. It would be a heroical and happy adventure for a lady to break the ice and provide an instance of one that has successfully overcome a tyrannical custom. The problem is that the fear of rejection has hindered many a fine attempt that way. Yet we see no reason why a woman that has sense enough to make a good choice . . . would be obliged to smother her love. On the contrary, it would be the best method to reveal it, since by that means she would soon either find a good reception or a cure, for we think it very unlikely a person would long love anyone that rejected them. [*AO*, 2:309]

Q. *In what way shall a shamefaced virgin let a person know she loves him?*

A. If the lady who proposed this question has either hands or eyes, she need not be taught how to use them, unless her spark is a fool or blind. [*AO*, 2:345]

Two women asked advice about how to attract particular men.

Q. *Gentlemen, I was (not long since) courted by a very sober young man and one that I think has an honest mind, but he had not come to me above two or three months before I was courted by another (who was newly come from sea, and had got him some fine clothes, and was more genteel than the former). He so took my fancy that I slighted the former and desired him not to come in my company, seeming to be displeased with him (when truly I had no cause). On that he very kindly told me that rather than be a hindrance to one he so well loved, he would stay away and bid me farewell. And now my genteel spark has left me, which makes me much repent that I ever put my former lover off. My friends have heard of it. They are very angry with me and say it was the worst day's work that ever I did. . . . I desire your directions, for I have tried the utmost of my skill already, by coming as often in his company as I conveniently can and likewise by my behavior in his company, such as smiling on him and using as many ways to express my mind to him as my modesty will allow of . . . yet all will not do. So now if you can give me directions that I may use to effect my desire, you will much oblige your humble servant.*

A. Poor compassionable creature! Send but your marks and name, and that of this hard-hearted former lover of yours, and we'll be sure to publish yours at least in one of our advertisements, with the doleful cause of your complaint and sad condition. If that doesn't melt him, sure his heart's as hard as an oak, and you must despair of winning him again. [Q3, 11:28, 14 October 1693]

Q. *I'm extremely in love with a young gentleman and have frequently gone to visit one of my friends, where I could see and be near him.*

I've twice written to him; he answered but said nothing of love.
I'm informed he's in love with another lady who lives near me,
though she knows nothing of it. If you could tell me how I could
prevail with him not to love her or prevail with her not to admit
his addresses, that would extremely oblige me.

A. And by obliging you probably we disoblige both of the others,
for gaining one friend can make ourselves two enemies.
However, ... since you first asked our assistance, you're welcome to the best advice we can give you. First find out if
the lady loves him in return. If she does and deserves him
it would be wrong to attempt to part them, and we won't
help in that effort. If she is not interested in him, make her
your confidant. If she's generous, she'll assist you in your
amour. Perhaps then she might treat her servant badly in
his presence, which could incline him to opt for a less tyrannical mistress. And you stand ready to take him into your
protection. [Q.1, 14:21, 31 July 1694]

Some men had questions about courtship behavior: What was
permissible? What was not?

Q. *Will a true lover offer any injury to a person he loves?*
A. We suppose this injury to be understood as being to her honor
and we answer it in the negative. . . . Respect is the very
essence of true love. Wherever then that respect ceases,
as it does with a vengeance when honor is attempted, the
love must necessarily cease together with it. By that very
offer the pretender changes the handsome name of a lover
into one much more frightful and horrid, or at least we
should think it so to anybody who but makes the slightest
pretenses to virtue. [Q.8, 2:13, 7 July 1691]

Q. *Are tears, sighs, and earnest entreaties of greater force to obtain a*
lady's favor than a moderate degree of zeal with a wise and manly
carriage?

A. There are few ladies who do not love to have an absolute power over their lovers. . . . Accordingly, for tears and all that, though a lover ought not to use them too freely, he ought perhaps to have a secret reserve of them to be at the lady's service if she desires it. Though we think on her side, too, it would be better not to put him to it and suffer her heart to be wrought upon by some less tedious method. [Q.4, 4:3, 6 October 1691]

Q. *Is interrupting discourse by repeated kisses rude and unmannerly and more apt to create aversion than love?*

A. Not so hasty, good sir! You have made great progress indeed in your amour. . . . The truth is, kissing is a luscious diet. . . . He must therefore remember to feed cautiously, as if he were eating melons. Moderation verily is an excellent thing, which he must observe . . . and kiss as well as talk, with discretion. [Q.5, 4:3, 6 October 1691]

Q. *A man has been in love for five years and never disclosed it to the gentlewoman because he fears a denial. She's somewhat older, but their fortunes are much alike. He can't lawfully marry in less than a year and fears his love's so violent he can't live so long without her. He being bashful desires your direction about how to reveal his passion to her.*

A. Lovers are ungovernable creatures! He'll think it very hard if we say he can't in honor tell the lady he loves her until he is able to marry, but it would be very impolitic to be too hasty and ruin the lady and himself too. If he addresses her too soon, that would make it easy for her to deny his suit. But let him be satisfied with her acquaintance and endeavor to deserve a particular share in her esteem without mentioning his love until it will be no injury to her to receive it. And we suppose a man that has sense enough to be in love and so constant has made a good choice, so consequently he need not fear a refusal. [Q.8, 6:27, 26 March 1692]

Some questions described interactions in groups of young people, some of which would be interpreted as disturbing today.

Q. *I am sometimes in company with honest young women and kiss them in a frolic, as others used to do. Query: Is this a sin or no?*
A. There's a civil kiss and an uncivil one. If the first, sure there's no hurt in them; if the latter, be your own judge. [Q.1, 15:24, 24 November 1694]

Q. *I am intimately acquainted with a young gentleman whose conversation is for the most part very diverting and witty. Sometimes, though, he speaks very lewdly. Query: Is it a sin to keep him company and participate in that lewd discourse?*
A. Yes, doubtless, if you don't reprove him for it or can any way avoid it. The consequences are dangerous and the more frequent the conversation the more mischievous. That is true especially when the poison is sweetened with wit, which is one of the most dangerous baits wherewith the devil destroys mankind. [Q.5, 17:27, 2 July 1695]

Q. *A certain young man gave a maid powder in her drink and caused her to follow him out of one room into another, kissing him before them all and not paying attention to anyone else in the room. Whence comes the strange power of these potions?*
A. If there be anything really effected it must be either by natural magic, some occult quality or other (the *je ne sais quoi* of the philosophers) or else plainly diabolical, or downright witchcraft. [Q.10, 18:1, 16 July 1695]

If the object of affection did not reciprocate with similar feelings, querists described anguish and despair—theirs or a friend's.

Q. *A young gentlewoman has been passionately in love for three or four years with a gentleman who was wholly ignorant of it until recently. But she has now ... not only written to him but also sent a messenger asking him to call on her. He did that twice, but ... declared he would have nothing to do with her. Still, she persists in her passion to such a degree that I'm afraid it will end in a desperate event, since there is no possibility of persuading the gentleman to marry her, for he has given good reasons to the contrary. As a friend of hers, I have given her the best advice I can to persuade her to desist from her passion, but without success. Therefore, I beg your advice for her, which I hope she will pay attention to.*

A. Her case is not singular.... There may indeed be good reasons for not reciprocating affection, such as a prior engagement or ... the disagreeableness of the person that loves them. But in such instances men ought to behave with as much goodness and compassion as possible, only slighting a woman enough to bring her to her senses.... His declaring that he'll have nothing to do with her is such a rude sort of answer as deserves her scorn.... Therefore, she must resolve to conquer her emotions and not to throw herself away. To encourage her in that undertaking, we'll assure her that we have known some persons who have succeeded in similar efforts.... She must adopt what will best occupy her mind, such as various sorts of diversions—company, plays, walks, dancing, singing, or any innocent mirth. And also more serious endeavors—work, reading, or devotion— never mentioning, or suffering to be mentioned, anything that relates to the gentleman, unless it insists on the impossibility of her ever having him. And if she'll take this course, we are sure that in half a year or less it will produce a happy effect. [Q3, 14:17, 17 July 1694]

Sometimes men described impediments to their courtship hopes and asked the Athenians' advice on circumventing them; the two below are unique. Perhaps a seemingly unrelated query about tobacco or coffee consumption helps to explain the second.

Q. *It is my misfortune to be red-haired.... I love a lady that has the greatest aversion imaginable to that colored hair. I have sufficient hope of obtaining her were that obstacle removed, but until it be, I dare not make my address.... I only beg you would direct me to a method as may make it brown for 15 or 16 days ... and then to repeat it again; for if she discovers it at any time after marriage, her aversion will be equally fatal to me as before.*

A. Some thousands perhaps for the same misfortune you complain of have cut off their hair and worn wigs of a more agreeable color, for which we think no wise man could blame them. Why can't you do the same, which by always keeping your head close shaved, might keep it a secret from the lady? ... However, if you are fixed not to part with it, ... we yet fancy it can't be impossible to have your hair stained or dyed by a skillful painter. [Q.2, 10:14, 13 May 1693]

Advertisement. A gentleman having sent a question to the Athenian Society how he may change his hair that is red to a brown color, their bookseller has since received information of a gentlewoman who has attained to great perfection in that as well as in many other secrets for the preserving and improving of beauty.... She prepares to color the hair of a very good brown or black (whichever shall be desired), so that it shall ... not come off with sweat or even with washing. She ... is to be spoken with near the King's bathhouse in Long Acre. [10:15, 16 May 1693]

Q. *I'm now courting a young lady who is very agreeable, her fortune and quality being equal to my birth and estate. But the problem is that she drinks an unsufferable amount of coffee, which I think is the reason for her coyness and aversion to my courtship. She has an aversion for me, and therefore I hope some way may be found to make her less cruel. I beg your advice in this matter.*

A. It's not likely we can persuade the lady not to drink this stygian liquor if you yourself have no power over her. We know only two ways. Either get some of her friends to tell her the dangerous effects of coffee in both sexes—that it will make her look old, spoil her teeth, and the like ... whereas chocolate will have the contrary effects for both sexes. Or if that does not work, drink excessive amounts of coffee yourself in front of her until you have topped her consumption. Resolve to drink it as long as she does. Then possibly she will be influenced by her pity for your circumstances and fear that such intemperance will injure you, bringing on some paralytical distemper. This is especially true if she intends to marry you, for she won't want to set you so poor an example. [Q3, 17:7, 23 April 1695]

Q. *Are coffee and tobacco prejudicial to reproduction, especially in the female sex?*

A. Both, moderately taken, are beneficial.... However, coffee to excess is very prejudicial to fertility. I knew a gentlewoman that drank much coffee and her children were imperfect, weak, and ill-shaped. Nature by the aforementioned excess ... was thereby much weakened for a perfect formation. [Q4, 1:23, undated, after 23 May 1691]

A man asked how to approach a young woman of higher status, one indication of which was her being accompanied by a Black servant, who might have been enslaved. The Athenians' jocular reply suggested they did not take the question seriously.

Q. *I must beg favor in this case. I have been seated next to a particular young lady at church. She ogles extremely at me. I am certain that she has a very considerable fortune by her appearance, because she has a black servant to wait upon her. Gentlemen, I have a handycrafts trade, and I dare not presume to approach her without your assistance. Please answer quickly.*

A. Take courage, man, the work's near done, she's half yours already. But before we are too confident, we must ask one civil question: Are the looks really directed at you? If you are not deceived and the daughter is gained, you must act honorably. Visit the father and tell him how much she loves you and that you are very willing to keep her from an asylum, which is not a common piece of generosity. You can say that you like her money as well as she can like your person, and that if he'll commit her to your care, you'll make a very civil sort of a husband. [Q.5, 17:19, 4 June 1695]

A brother tried to help his sister's suitor, but instead injured his cause.

Q. *A gentleman with a large estate, sober and moderate but in truth not particularly shrewd, courted a sister of mine. She rejected his offers, chiefly because of several unfortunate expressions he had made in his visits and letters. Being aware of that problem, he asked me (who was willing to agree to the match) to give him a rough draft of some letters. I accordingly did that, and from time to time he sent them to her. However, by comparing them with his former letters, she discovered or at least suspected the cheat and has now quite cast him off. Pray let me know . . . was it a fault in me to write those letters?*

A. You have been the accidental cause, and so are a hundred others, of such mischief as they are not to answer for.... We think it was a piece of kindness in you to the sister, rather than a fault, to write the letters. [Q.2, 14:25, 14 August 1694]

Both men and women wondered about the limits on courtship behavior and the consequences if those limits were breached.

Q. *A gentleman, by a thousand oaths and protestations to a lady, declared that he would be unhappy and miserable if she did not permit his passion. He vowed if she granted it, he would be eternally true to none but her. She out of gratitude and goodness at last granted it. . . . But this perfidious man was no sooner sure of his conquest than he slighted what before he adored and died for. Now the lady by too great an act of generosity has removed his misery to herself.... Query: Can he marry another or is there any way to reclaim him?*

A. No, he cannot lawfully marry anyone but that lady. But that result will be no satisfaction to you, for we may without injustice affirm that he who can be base enough to betray so much goodness will never attend to his duty or conscience, if he has any.... Therefore, you are now bravely to resolve and conquer yourself by reason. You'll undoubtedly find more happiness that way than in anything else. [Q.9, 6:25, 26 March 1692]

Q. *I'm a young gentleman almost of age. I have for some time made honorable love to a young and beautiful lady. I have made all the advances in her favor that consist with virtue and honor ... but must acknowledge when I'm alone with my mistress ... it's impossible but that my burning lips must give me all the effects as warm love and young blood can inspire—Nay, those ideas often carry me so far as to ... anticipate what's yet to come upon my pillow.... Now I desire your opinion: Are these dalliances or the last transport of thought a sin?*

A. To this we answer that ... you will unavoidably conclude that there's no sin in consummation itself before marriage.... But if we sin before marriage, marriage cannot transform a past act that otherwise would be sin into none. In fact, every act is sin or no sin as soon as completed. [Q.3, 9:28, 18 March 1693]

Q. *I desire to know (for it concerns me) how a woman ought to behave herself with a man who has made attempts against her honor? If she treats him civilly ... does she not transgress the rules of decency? ... On the other side, ... if she refuses ... to let him see her, does she not disobey that Christian law of forgiving injuries?*

A. The securest way is to avoid your seducer, nor can you prudently admit of any intimacy with him after, for how can

you expect that either you or virtue should prevail with
him, when by such an offer he has tacitly declared he values
neither?... If you can be charitable enough to make a husband of him... avoid seeing him except in some company
and marry as fast as you can.... Though we ought to forgive
our enemy,... we are not obliged to... put it again in his
power to affront or injure us. [Q5, 12:16, 16 December 1693]

Correspondents asked for advice when courtships went awry.
Sometimes the Athenians jocularly implied (as in the second
answer below) that the relationships might not turn out as well
as the lovers expected.

Q. *I some time ago contracted an entire friendship with a particular
person, which I hoped would not have expired before our lives, but
I find myself greatly mistaken, for I am without any cause very
much slighted.... For that reason I have no peace day or night.... I
earnestly request you would be pleased to advise me speedily what
I shall do.*

A. If it be a woman, you may conclude that she has no regard
for you.... Slighting you is the highest contempt.... You
must practice to slight her, that's the remedy. [Q6, 8:19, 1
November 1692]

Q. *A friend of mine often importuned me to make my addresses to
a lady, young, beautiful, and witty, assuring me that if I should
approve of her, it lay in his power to procure her consent to marry
me. I readily consented and accordingly made her a visit. I was
received with abundance of respect,... which I have often done
with the same success. Lately, without any provocation she has
banished me from her presence....*

*Now I find she is in love with my friend and to oblige him
allowed my visits.... To be plain, I am desperately in love with
her, she as much with my friend. I court her and she solicits him,
though both are equally successless, for he to my knowledge loathes*

her as much as I love her. I know not how to behave myself in this intricate business. Your speedy advice will oblige a poor despairing lover.

A. If the lady is resolute against seeing you, it may be better to absent yourself for a while, . . . but taking care to let her know that it's in obedience to her severe commands that you violate your own inclinations. . . . In the meanwhile she has not forbidden you writing to her, . . . therefore be sure to ply her well with letters. . . . And if you can, get some friend of hers to espouse your cause, for then she's half yours. At the same time prevail with the gentleman who brought you into these sad circumstances plainly to let the lady know he can't love her. Nay, rather than fail, to affront her—tell her her breath stinks, or that she's ugly, and if that won't do, she's incurable. If this works, then strike while the iron's hot, and be the humblest, doting, whining spaniel-thing that ever lay on a lady's petticoats, . . . and this way, if any, the lady may chance to love you, and make you unhappy. [Q.1, II:18, 9 September 1693]

Q. *I have loved and courted a gentlewoman above three years. She ever gave me kind entertainment and never refused my company, but accepted all kindness from me. But when I proposed marriage to her, she would tell me I was too young yet. She put me off with such slight excuses but still kept me company, until of late she has fallen off suddenly without any manner of cause or reason of offense from me. She denies me her company and will not suffer me to see her nor speak to her, which makes me very melancholy and discontented. She professes a great deal of religion and Christianity, but of late she acts like a heathen to me, though I never gave her any cause. Your speedy advice in this uneasy condition is earnestly desired.*

A. Would you know the disease or the remedy? Perhaps you are poorer than she is, or she has a richer or more agreeable person that offers. However, she has not dealt handsomely with you to entertain you so long and discard you at last. These accidents are so common in both sexes that it's in vain to complain of them or reproach one another. For remedy, forget her as she does you. In order to do it, get another mistress. [Q.2, II:28, 14 October 1693]

Q. *I had the misfortune to have a young gentleman fall in love with me to such a degree that he became distracted and died. Now since I could not love him, though his person and estate were much finer than I could expect, I can't be satisfied until you have passed your judgment about whether I have a great deal to answer for in his death. The truth is that I never gave him any encouragement to continue his addresses, so neither did I much slight him. Yet since I've heard of his death, I find myself extremely dissatisfied. Pray give me your resolution as speedily as possible.*

A. If it was from a natural cruelty or vanity that you slighted the gentleman's passion and were the unhappy cause of his distraction and death, you are very criminal and should severely repent it.... If you found a natural aversion and antipathy against him in your mind,... you might however pity his fate, as the softness and goodness of your sex requires you to do. If things were as you represent them, that you did not slight or affront him and yet he would despair and die without any provocation, it was his own fault and you are not at all criminal in the matter. [Q.4, II:28, 14 October 1693]

Q. *I am a young woman who has been courted by several very good gentlemen, but I never could love any of them. Then it was my hard fortune to be courted by a master of a ship, and I loved him as dearly as my life. When he knew I loved him, he would have lain with me, but as dearly as I loved him I kept myself honest. He saw that he could not make a whore of me, told me he loved me for my virtue, and did it only to try me. So I could not hate him. All this was against my friends' consent, so that they turned me*

*out of their doors because I loved him. Then he promised to marry
me and I lent him money.*

*The night before we were to be married, he went away and I
have not seen him since. Pray be pleased to advise me what to do.
Had I best marry another or live a maid all my lifetime, or send
letters to him, kind words or cross words for revenge? He has not
sent one word since he went away and my heart is almost broken.
Your speedy answer is desired.*

A. Once a year we meet with such innocence and when we do
we inform the world of it. By entertaining a faithless sailor
against your friends' consent, you behaved badly and might
have been more severely punished than you have been. It's
good you came off as well you did, and that your love and
innocence together have not quite ruined you.... We believe you escaped well with the loss of a little money when
he left you your virtue, which was much more valuable.

Now to answer your questions: Admit some other more
virtuous and deserving lover, if any such offers, which will
be the best way to put the traitor out of your memory....
As for letters to him, never trouble yourself, since either
he'll not answer them at all ... or else wheedle you again,
make a thousand excuses (which we men never lack), and
ten to one persuade you to believe him and give him all he
had left behind. Or if he should marry you, he might have
two or three wives in other ports, who must all be served
before you. [Q3, 12:24, 12 January 1694]

Q. *A young man from the city made his addresses to a country gentlewoman for nearly a year and gained her affections. But afterward
he slighted her without any explanation. She is a very beautiful and
virtuous lady who has been and is still in love with him to such a
degree that her life is despaired of. Is this gentleman, knowing he
is the cause of her illness, obliged to marry her in conscience? And
if he does not and she dies, is he guilty of her death?*

A. He is obliged in honor and conscience to marry her, but we think the lady happier without him than she could be with such an inconstant lover. She should consider that it's better for her to discover his nature now than make herself ill. [Q3, 14:2, 26 May 1694]

Q. *I was lately courting a lady who was said to have a great fortune. After so long an acquaintance that she found I really loved her, she revealed to me that she had no fortune. I really loved her and could not withdraw myself suddenly but endeavored it by degrees. I have at last pretty well conquered my passion. But now I find she is in love with me, caused by my loving her. I have convincing proof it's no deceit. I have a small estate, but not enough to maintain us both in the manner in which we were raised. Since I have been the occasion for her passion, which she says she shall never forgo, tell me if I ought to marry her or leave her in that condition.*

A. The lady has acted very honorably in revealing the truth to you, although she did not act prudently in passing for what she was not. . . . Had she carried on the design to perfection and married anyone who believed she had a fortune, it might have caused continual disquiets between them when they learned of the deception. And so in your case she owes the unhappiness more to the deceit than to you. You are undoubtedly free to act as you please, if you made her no promises after you knew she had nothing. But if you did, they are as binding as if she really had what you first expected. [Q5, 15:3, 11 September 1694] [AO, 2:288]

Q. *A gentleman fell in love with a young lady. After he disclosed himself to her with all kindness, she slighted him and never would admit she had any respect for him. He, observing that, let it fall and minded it no more, she agreeing it should be so as well as he. Now another young lady is in love with this gentleman and professes herself to be wholly his, if he will remain constant. He considers this and begins to court her. The former, hearing this, charges him with inconstancy. Now your judgment in both cases is required; which of them should he cleave to?*

A. You are obliged to keep to the last, having already made your addresses to her and handsomely retreated from the first. [*AO*, 2:183]

Men asked about dealing with rivals, both friends and not.

Q. *Two friends see the same lady in the same day, the first bringing the second to see her, asking his advice, and desiring his assistance in the amour—He, on his seeing her, falls also desperately in love with her—Which of the two in this case ought to desist? And if both address her, is their friendship thereby actually dissolved and ruined?*

A. It would be generous if . . . he that saw her last would for that reason give up all to his friend. . . . We believe it next to impossible their friendship could be long-lived, but the only way . . . is for both to continue their addresses fairly and handsomely, without any reflections or derogation by one of the other, and to leave the decision to the lady herself or lady fortune. [Q3, 3:13, 8 September 1691]

Q. *I contracted a friendship of the strictest kind and highest degree with a young lady, who is (without flattery) one of the noblest of her sex. Our passions, fortunes, and everything else were equal. We seemed designed for each other, yet if there is such a thing as platonic love, that was all that possessed our souls. . . . But my business calling me to Spain (where I continued about a year), we were forced to part, though with grief to both. . . . Nothing could satisfy me until my return, when as soon as I saw her, I threw myself into her arms, expressing the highest passion I was capable of.*

She, surprised at my behavior, was silent for a while, but then received me with a sigh, telling me her parents had promised her to another person. Although she loved me, thinking I did not feel the same she had given her consent, and they were to be married within a month.

To make a long story short, after some conversation I left her,
and then happily met my rival in a private field. I told him our
circumstances and endeavored to argue him out of marrying her.
When that failed, I drew and told him he must fight me or quit
his pretensions to her. We fought. I wounded and disarmed him,
but gave him his life, which he reciprocated by surrendering his
right in her to me. He quitted her without revealing the reason, so
I openly courted her and gained her parents' consent. Now I am in
expectations of the happy day, and I would know of you:
  Q.1. *Is there or can there be such a thing as platonic love?*
  Q.2. *Did I do ill in fighting my rival, because if I had not done that*
        we all three would have been made miserable?
A.1. The idea of platonic love now is mostly confined to an uncommon love, viz., that between two different sexes, which
if it had been between two of the same sex, might be well
expressed as friendship. That there is such a thing we have
several instances to convince us....
A.2. Yes, certainly, we are forbidden to do ill that good may
come of it. It's a bad act to assault any person, except in
one's own just defense, and comes close to murder. We
wish you as much happiness in your marriage as you promise yourself, but we don't understand how any gentleman
can lose his right to anything because another has a longer
sword. [Q.4, 7:13, 10 May 1692]

  Q. *A gentleman courts a lady of a considerable fortune and has gained*
      her affections and friends' consent to be married.... I have too
      much reason to suspect his honesty as to women. Query: Am I
      obliged to acquaint the lady's friends therewith?... I'm the more
      cautious of acting in the case lest it should savor of interest or envy,
      there having been some recent overtures of marriage between her
      parents and myself.
  A. If you love the lady, it's fair play between rivals...to ruin his
      reputation with the old folks.... You ought however to

consider, supposing your intelligence certain, whether the accusation is grounded on single instances or a confirmed habit. If the latter, you're undoubtedly obliged to let the family know it. If only the former, we are not so sure of it. [Q.7, 10:7, 18 April 1693]

Q. *A friend of mine has desired me to propose the following case to you and request your speedy advice in it. He has long courted a young lady but without any success. He has lately learned that she rejects his addresses because she loves another person, whose whole circumstances are in every way inferior to his. Her parents . . . would be extremely grieved if she should marry the other man. Yet I believe she will do that if her parents don't stop her, although in all appearance such a marriage will lead to her misery and ruin. Query: Should my friend, who is the only one who knows these intrigues, tell her parents and thereby do what he can to prevent that marriage? Or how should he act . . . consistent with prudence, honor, and conscience?*

A. It's very hard for your friend, he being so nearly concerned in the affair, to make a disinterested judgment. . . . If he'll be both honest and kind to his mistress, too, he must acquaint some one of her friends that is wise enough to prevail with her . . . not to be hasty in marrying or engaging too far without the advice and consent of her parents. . . . And in the meanwhile let this friend . . . advise her to be cautious and let them also find out his imperfections. . . . And as for yourself, you must not be too often in her company, nor importune her too much with your passion, but sometimes let her know you still esteem her. . . . If possible, keep her ignorant that you know anything of the marriage plans. If this method won't do, we can think of none you can take that will be either for her or your happiness. . . . If the best you can hope is that her parents should by their influence over her compel her to marry you, you can never expect the affections of a woman so gained. [Q.3, 11:21, 19 September 1693]

Q. *A young gentlewoman, fair and virtuous, witty and good natured, with honor enough, is at her mother's and her own disposal. I have had strong inclinations for some time to accost her as her lover. But I am informed there is another who has for a long time offered his service to her, as I hear without much success. Now I beg your advice if I may proceed in my design in honor and justice to this first pretender. If you think I may fairly go on, pray what methods may be likely to gain her? But if not, what virtuous actions may I probably take with one not altogether so virtuous nor handsome, nor of so benign a temperament? Your former answers in the* Mercury *have heightened my abhorrence of those impure freedoms which too many have used in such affairs.*

A. Your mistress's qualifications are enough to create many rivals, if you had none before; but if you had ten thousand, you have as fair a claim to court her as they. The outcome will be determined either by her or her friends. The best method to gain a virtuous wise woman is to do nothing that may render you mean and despicable either to her or to others.

You should give her sufficient testimonies of your passion to convince her that it is not only strong but lasting. You must base it chiefly on such of her qualifications as time can never efface: not on beauty, which is but a flash, but on prudence, generosity, and sweetness of disposition. With those qualities, nothing but death can put a period to your esteem. And as for your endeavoring to gain another, we think it not worth your while, for virtue and a good disposition are absolutely necessary in an agreeable wife. Without these good graces, your goddess will become a Harpy and soon devour all your quiet and happiness. [Q.3, 12:4, 11 November 1693]

Q. *Is fighting a duel for a mistress against laws divine and human, and so magistrates should take notice of such events, even if no death results?*

A. For one man to covet the blood of another is very unnatural and consequently a breach of his duty. Dueling for any reason is a most rash, foolish, and wicked thing, and no better than wishing the death of him they challenge.... But it does not concern magistrates to call men to account for their thoughts and intentions, and where there is no life lost, there's no injury done to the public, whatsoever the parties might design. [Q.4, 12:11, 28 November 1693]

Q. *It was my fortune to fall passionately in love with a young lady, who for a long time treated me very indifferently, but persevering I at length made her aware of my love and received some small assurance of hers. I described my amour to a friend who seemed to deride it as my folly.... But he took that opportunity to ingratiate himself with her, showing her all the diversions imaginable.... He has by these means and by giving me a negative character, which I do not deserve, deprived me of all my hopes for the future. Therefore, I desire to know: First, what must I do to regain the lady? Second, how should I deal with my supposed friend?*

A. First, let her know by letter or special messenger how you have been abused and by whom. Let her know that it has been in your friend's interest to deceive her . . . and ask only the favor of being permitted to speak for yourself.... Second, make him honest if you can, by endeavoring to convince him how dishonorably he has dealt with you. Tell him that he can only compensate you and acquit himself by confessing to the lady.... He should beg both your pardons and support your courtship. If he won't do this, you have no way but to make the best use of his perfidy by being careful whom you trust in your amours another time. [Q.6, 12:20, 30 December 1693]

Q. *I have lost a young lady's affections, along with a considerable for-tune, through the treachery of a pretended bosom friend. He, being familiar with her family, has given her several forged letters in my name. She has now treated me so badly that I despair of recovering my interest in her. Please advise me how I should punish him and recover her favor.*

A. It would be best if this bosom friend of yours (a he-friend we hope) is not himself in love with the lady. If he is, your best revenge will be to undeceive and marry her, but the question is how you shall accomplish that. If you can't speak with her, you must write to her and vindicate yourself or get some better friend than the first to do that for you. [Q5, 16:26, 16 March 1695]

Some men were involved with more than one woman and asked for advice on dealing with them. One "old maid" similarly sought advice about her suitors.

Q. *I am a young man and am acquainted with two young ladies. I have courted the one and the other I can plainly see loves me. But she against her own inclinations pleads for me to marry the other and uses all her interest to make me happy, although I fear she will thereby be unhappy. Query: Which of the two ought I to marry, she whom I have courted or the other that loves me?*

A. If the person you have courted either slights or has no es-teem for you, you may without any prejudice put an end to your suit. If you have generosity and gratitude enough to love where you are beloved, probably you will not only make yourself happy but another also. If on the contrary the lady you have made your addresses to accepts and has made a positive return to them, you can neither in justice nor honor forsake her, but must be hers. You can only afford the poor suffering other lady a little cold pity. [Q5, 12:19, 26 December 1693]

Q. *I've had affection for a virtuous young lady for these two years, but have not seen her this year and half, being at a great distance from her. I never disclosed my passion to her until four months ago. I've always continued constant to her, not having had the least thoughts of any other. Yet about nine months since I courted another lady (whom I could not love), merely for diversion. She accepted my courtship and thereupon I promised her marriage.*

However, I'm assured my friends won't consent to a match, her fortune being far inferior to mine, though the former lady's is equal to mine. I am assured of my friends' consent to that marriage. Besides, my own inclination is still fixed on her only. Query: Can I break my promise to her to whom I have so great an aversion and marry the other, whom I still so passionately love?

A. First, you must ask the loved lady whether she'll have you, and secondly, the lady that's hated, whether she will part with you. Your declaration to the former does not amount to a promise and therefore cannot clear you from the latter. If you forsake the second without her consent and marry the first, you cannot expect to live happy. Even though men fancy heaven laughs at lovers' perjuries or does not regard them at all, we know no privilege suitors have to lie any more than others.... The examples are so frequent that one would think the credulous female sex should take more care whom they believed. [Q.6, 14:26, 18 August 1694] [*AO*, 2:157]

Q. *Not long ago I fell passionately in love with a virtuous, well-descended lady of equal age and fortune to myself. I wrote to her to tell her of my passion. But she had no sooner received the letter than she rejected my offer. She ... avoided me as much as possible, being at the same time courted by a young gentleman much above my fortune, who continued his courtship for about two months. In the end she declined his courtship, slighted him, and sent for me. She showed me all his letters, telling me if I'd prove constant she'd be eternally mine. But less than a week afterward I had another proposal made me from a virtuous and beautiful young lady who has a much greater fortune and is as well educated as the former. Now I desire your advice (and resolve to be governed by it). Can I justly and honorably embrace the better offer and reject the former, there never having been any absolute promise between us, for my inclinations are much more for the latter?*

A.   If you did not engage yourself to the first, there's no reason why you should not embrace the more advantageous proposals of the latter. But by saying that you made no absolute promise, you seem to imply that some sort of promise was made, and it's also probable that you responded positively to her later obliging offer. If you did that and she understood it as accepting her offer, we think that you can't honorably get clear of the first engagement. [Q.1, 16:24, 9 March 1695]

Q.   *I am an old maid, 30 years of age. This is a state I always dreaded, and I . . . cannot tell why fortune should be more unkind to me than she has been to the rest of my relations. I have only attracted a tailor, a weaver, and a journeyman shoemaker. I have a great aversion to all those trades. Even so, I would not have refused them all, except for my greater love for a barber who used to honor me with his company a little now and then. But now that he recognizes that I am in love with him, he has stopped visiting me. He also avoids my company at all places where I go in hopes of seeing him.*

    Now, gentlemen, my request is that you would please advise me what I should do about him. . . . Otherwise I must be forced to choose someone in one of the aforementioned trades or at least the first that comes to me. . . . Neither am I someone to avoid, having two trades, viz., the art of Japanning and periwig making. In addition, I have 30 or 40£ in ready money and a lottery ticket.

A.   Marry as fast as you can, repent, and then grow wiser. [Q.2, 17:10, 4 May 1695]

Sometimes men sought friendship rather than courtship and complications ensued. One woman did not want to marry anyone, including a man who had courted her.

Q. *A gentleman though married made his addresses to a young lady, concealing his marriage and not designing anything dishonorable. He acted purely out of a desire to gain her acquaintance, for he was charmed by her conversation. His wife died some time ago and he is now extremely melancholy. . . . Being censured by her relations for his former intrigue during his marriage and dissuaded by his own friends from entertaining any thoughts of love, it's feared that he will make some desperate attempt upon himself. Your advice, therefore gentlemen, is speedily desired. . . . May the young lady without any reflection upon her honor entertain him, notwithstanding his former fault (as they are pleased to term it), provided his person, fortune, etc., be not disagreeable?*

A. This is a very uncommon relation, but if it is the utmost that has passed, we think both the querist and the lady may proceed honorably enough to the highest bond of friendship. [Q3, 4:23, undated, after 28 November 1691]

Q. *Gentlemen, when I came into this country I addressed myself to a young lady of great merit without any other design than to spend some agreeable moments in her conversation. I have enjoyed all the pleasures of wit and good humor for above 6 months, and . . . she now reveals the most violent passion for me. Although I esteem her infinitely, I can't love her enough to make her my wife. I am at a loss what to do. I would not disoblige her, much less reduce her to despair, and yet I can't resolve to love her. Gentlemen, if you please to assist me with your good advice in the affair, you will do me a very sensible favor.*

A. We thought it convenient to put the substance of this letter in English, that no one might be at a loss for its meaning. [The question begins in French.] Our answer is that if the gentleman can't be won by so much merit nor respond to so great passion as . . . she has for him, he should treat her as honorably as he can. He should tell her the truth that he should be very happy in her friendship, but in a nearer relation he can't. . . . If this won't do, make fewer visits, and if that also proves successless, you may honorably . . . break off all pretensions for any further visits. This we think a much more honorable and fair method than any little idle excuses, which are frequently made in such cases. [Q.2, 8:22, 12 November 1692]

Q. *I have been intimately acquainted with an honest young woman in whose company I have much delighted. I am sure she fancies I will marry her, although she cannot expect it from anything that I have said. Query: Now that I know her expectations, is it unsuitable for a Christian to continue our relationship as before, since I have no plan to marry her? If this is impermissible, in what way?*

A. You ought to undeceive her. If after that she is content with your company, you may very innocently converse together. But it's likely that it will be difficult for her to continue your conversation upon such terms if she has expected the contrary. [Q.4, 14:2, 26 May 1694]

Q. *I am a virgin (at least I pass for such). It was my fortune about a year ago to meet a gentleman who honorably courted me until he had gained my heart and all my affection. But the unalterable resolution I have taken of living and dying a maid has hindered me from consenting to marry him. I forced him to promise me faithfully that he would never again visit me. But I . . . find I can never be happy without sometimes seeing him, whom I still love . . . though with nothing but a platonic passion. How may I regain his lost affection and keep a friendly correspondence with him, without doing anything that may . . . raise a scandal upon my reputation?*

A. Become a little more reasonable and admit your error. . . . Consider the true cause of this unhappiness, which is certainly love. . . . Before you can expect to be happy, you must know truly what you desire. If your resolutions remain unal-

terable, we'd advise you not to perplex the gentleman with
such a ridiculous love. . . . But if you can be reconciled to
matrimony, let him know it by the most prudent means. . . .
Or employ a secret friend to do it for you. Your reputation
will not be injured by retracting such an error as resolving
never to marry when you were too young to know better.
[Q.1, 18:20, 21 September 1695]

Men asked for advice in interpreting women's behavior and
women asked the same about men.

Q. *It has been my fortune to fall in love with a lady to whom I was
introduced. She seemed by all outward appearance to be as willing for a meeting as I. I have been once or twice in her company
but said nothing about my feelings for her. The last time I went,
I was told by a person who knew her that if I hoped to court her, I
was mistaken. You may very well guess how great my dejection
was when I heard my doom. Not long after, when I happened
to see her, methought she gave me some very kind looks and
some amorous glances. From those I concluded that what I was
told either did not come from her, or if it did her mind was now
altered, and she would be willing to receive my courtship. Now
I desire to know your sentiments of the matter, and if I ought to
proceed. I stand upon thorns every moment until I receive an
answer to my query.*

A. What a coward are you in love! There's very few conquests
of this nature that do not encounter several repulses before
the castle is stormed. Courage, man, and try your fortune!
Fortune helps the bold. If you're a true lover, you can't despair at a little hardship. [Q.5, 6:26, 26 March 1692]

Q. *It has been my fortune to fall in love with a young gentlewoman. Soon
after it happened we have been a fortnight in one house together
in the country. I have had frequent opportunities of making my
addresses to her. After a short time I found her by all her actions
to have the like passion for me, although . . . she in words gives me*

an absolute denial. . . . Her kisses are reciprocal when we are alone, and all other freedoms which consist with modesty and religion are permitted. Yet she affirms she does not love me so much as to make me her husband, nor ever will. Now I . . . not knowing how to take it (and lovers being commonly a little impatient), your speedy answer is earnestly desired. Should her words or her actions be esteemed the sentiments of her heart?

A. You write like a youngster in these affairs. . . . A little strangeness, only a few visits or a pretended voyage (which you may allege you are forced to by her unkindness) will set all to rights and bring her to speak as she thinks. . . . In some cases there's need enough of great caution and prudence, the inconstancy, levity, and prejudices of our own sex being so very notorious. [Q.3, II:9, 8 August 1693]

Q. *A young woman has been for some time courted very passionately by one of whom she has a very favorable opinion. The chief objection she has against him is that she thinks he has a bad disposition. She has tested him several ways, but he's too politic to reveal himself. Therefore, she desires you would show her a method in which she may find out the truth in a matter which so nearly concerns the happiness of her life.*

A. A very knotty business this, and we can't very well tell whether there's more than one infallible way to clear it. Marry him, and you will know what his disposition is less than half a year after. . . . But if you think that a desperate remedy, we'll advise you to make trial of some others. . . . Inquire of his long and familiar acquaintances. Observe how he behaves himself to his inferiors or how he looks when he loses at play, and not to you. . . . But if he happens to see this *Mercury,* look to yourself, lest he discover your character rather than you his. [Q.3, II:18, 9 September 1693]

Q. *I had the misfortune to commence an acquaintance with a young gentlewoman whose conversation proved so very agreeable that it created in me an extraordinary passion for her. She seemed to feel the same way. Many letters reciprocally passed between us to our mutual satisfaction. Recently, though, she urgently requested that I burn her letters, which at last to gratify her I did. She was no sooner assured of their destruction but contrary to all the promises she made she now receives me coldly. This makes me so very melancholy that I fear it will be my ruin. I have endeavored to behave with her with similar indifference and lately I took my final leave from her. But still I find it impossible to forget her and I cannot bear her absence, although I have been very sharply repulsed. I would desire your advice in the matter, being naturally prone to revenge, which must either fall on her or on myself.*

A. If you'll but wait a little, the work will effectually be done.... Seek out some more soft and gentle creature in whose looks you may find a sufficient balm for all your wounds. Never go near the first, unless it is as an old acquaintance to let her know the good success you have had with the second woman. This will please her well, since we naturally love to see others preferred before us. [Q.4, 16:30, 30 March 1695]

Q. *After an intimate acquaintance with a lady of quality and considerable fortune, and by frequent and familiar expressions of uncommon favors, I was induced to believe she offered more than ordinary kindness. So I at last declared my amorous affection. But when I revealed my intention, she seemed to scorn my proposals with the greatest regret and disdain imaginable. Even so, she continues a strict and kind correspondence, so long as I do not mention or send any letter tending to my former address....*

Yet I am informed of her uneasiness and melancholy temper when I am gone and of the pleasure and satisfaction she takes when I am talked of or am in company with her. Likewise, our daily, long, private, and single conversations ... confirm me in the belief ... that she loves me extremely well. Now, being fully assured I shall never gain her consent or prevail upon her by express courtship, and knowing that she is a lady of honor and entire chastity, I desire your opinion, what tacit method shall I use to marry her, without either speaking or writing to her of love and affection?

A. First of all, we congratulate your happiness in having a mistress that won't put you to the expenses of oaths or lies,
or so much as pen, ink, and paper. Indeed, we suspect you
don't know your own good fortune. Why, how many silly
things are we poor militant lovers obliged to say to our
mistresses before we can thoroughly deceive them?... All
this is clear gains to you. . . . Now for a little direction. . . .
Can't you love her in her own way and let her love which
way she pleases?... Only to sit still and be loved one would
think should be no very difficult matter.

   If you must say nothing, can't you look as well as think
the more? Nay, can't you speak too sideways, though you
may not speak directly? And good speed is often made by
sailing upon a side wind. Thus, you may insensibly gain
upon her. . . . In the meantime, be patient, observant, sub-
missive; and if this method gets her, be sure you don't forget
to send us word when you are married, that we may come
and dance at your wedding. [*AO*, 2:276–77]

CHAPTER 2

"Much Love and Moderate Conveniency"

CHOOSING A SPOUSE

AFTER A SUCCESSFUL COURTSHIP, couples moved toward marriage. But that process could be complicated. Some men and women seriously or jokingly asked the Athenians whom they should marry. A few described prospective spouses in broadly satirical terms, which the Athenians gleefully welcomed in the same spirit. More earnestly, other querists requested the Athenians' advice on property considerations, marriage ceremonies, or religion, among other topics.

Q. *Is it permissible to marry a person one cannot love in compliance to relations and to get an estate?*

A. We sometimes see persons love tenderly after marriage who could hardly endure each other's sight before.... But as it's proposed here, whether we may marry such as we cannot love, the question must be answered in the negative, since such a practice would be the most cruel and imprudent thing in the world. Society is the main end of marriage; love is the bond of society; and without love neither pleasure, profit, or honor can be found in marriage. He then or she that marry for so base an end as profit without any possibility or prospect of love is guilty of the highest brutality imaginable.... As one wittily observes, it is too general a truth to be feared that he who marries a woman he could never love will soon love a woman he never married. [Q.2, 1:13, 5 May 1691]

Q. *Are most matches in this age made for money?*
A. Both in this age and in all others, ... it's gold that has been the truest charm to procure love or at least the chain that has tied persons together without it. [Q.8, 1:13, 5 May 1691]

Q. *Why are widows more forward to marry than maids?*
A. Because ... the young fellows take it for granted, that it is nothing but—Up and Ride—and indeed almost ravish the widows into matrimony, if they have any appurtenances worth angling for. This for the men's side—then for the women's.... Which of the two is the easier to mount, an old hack that has been beating upon the road this ten year or a young skittish filly that was never ridden before? [Q.6{7}, 4:13, 10 November 1691]

Q. *Is it better to marry a woman with a singular good disposition and not truly religious or a woman of a crabbed disposition that is religious?*
A. For the first, there are hopes of her, if she is of a good disposition.... She may improve and by God's mercy become truly pious and religious.... A good man might live more comfortably with her than the other, ... who after all may be mistaken in her piety, howsoever much she pretends to it. [Q.9{10}, 4:13, 10 November 1691]

Q. *Who are wisest, those that marry for love or for convenience?*
A. They are both fools if they marry for one without the other. Love without the necessary conveniences of life will soon wear threadbare. Conveniences without love are no better than being chained to a post for the sake of a little meat, drink, and clothing. But much love and moderate conveni-

ency are far better than the most plentiful estate with little or no love. [Q.3, 5:3, 8 December 1691]

Q. *I am a bachelor and have an estate which I am very desirous should descend to one of my own blood. I would marry for that reason, but if I have no children by my wife, is my marriage void because procreation is the end of marriage?*

A. But what if it should be your own fault?... And are there not other ends of marriage beside what you assign?... We think you'd do better unmarried. [Q.2, 11:1, 11 July 1693]

Q. *Is it permissible for a woman to marry one she does not love in hopes that love will come after?*

A. There's a great deal of difference between not loving a person and not being able to love him because of an unconquerable aversion to him.... We think in that case it's not prudent nor permissible to marry because one main end of matrimony, mutual comfort and support, can never be achieved. Besides, you'll find so much to bear with and forgive in your husband, as well as he in you, that unless you are both angels, without this love on both sides to sweeten and soften, all you are like to lead is a miserable life. But, to tell the truth, men are seldom so accommodating after marriage as before, so ten to one you must do all yourself toward loving them, since they generally think they have said their part before matrimony. [Q.7, 15:26, 1 December 1694] [AO, 2:482]

When a female correspondent asserted she did not want to marry, the Athenians adopted an unusual tactic: interpolating comments in her question as well as offering their usual reply.

Q. *A person who is not interested in marriage [that may be] thinks herself very happy [she knows we can't disprove her] and is extremely obsessed with the fear of a bad husband [but is not a bad house better than no house at all?]. She desires to know if being an old maid is really so great a bugbear, fearing that fate should oblige her to marry against all sense and reason.*

A.   O! such a terrible bugbear that you never saw anything like it!... The very approach of such a creature has frightened many a good virgin out of her wits and into matrimony. The querist... must neither hearken to any huge-he-sirens that would snap her up as a morsel and digest her and her fortunes before the year's at an end, nor yet remain so long unmarried that the market will be ended and she left upon her own hands. [Q.6, 16:26, 16 March 1695] [*AO*, 2:243]

When male and female correspondents requested the Athenians' advice on whom to marry, sometimes the questions appeared to be serious but at other times were clearly jocular, receiving reciprocal witty treatment. The Athenians did respond with care to a brother who wanted to select a husband for his sister, reading between the lines of the query to support the young woman's obvious preference.

Q.   *My parents dying in my infancy left me in the care of friends for my education,... but now I'm of age,... I must look to myself. I... have several pretenders. The most eager a good, honest tradesman who is well settled in the world, though I find not overstocked with sense. Another a sparkish fellow that says he's an author, nay a poet, too, as I find to my sorrow, for he generally pesters me once a day with some doleful sonnet or other.... There's a third... a rich old graceless piece of quality, that whenever he sees me is ready to devour me and promises me a considerable settlement if I'll consent to be his. I must speedily resolve upon one thing or other and therefore desire your advice as soon as possible.*

A.   To begin then, for luck's sake, with your scribbling lover, we find, Madam, you write a very good hand and an indifferent style and may for those reasons be a proper helpmeet for such a sort of a mortal. We tell you that... one poor author, without something else to live upon, can never maintain a family.... For your old lecher of quality, who ... would have you his ... whore, we hope there's no need to advise you against him.... Our sage advice is clearly for the honest tradesman, who will maintain you answerably to his and your quality, and if he doesn't have perhaps as much sense as some of his neighbors, ... will make the more obedient husband—and so, well may you do together. [Q.1, 10:9, 25 April 1693]

Q. *I'm a young woman and would, like others, get as good a husband as possible. How should I choose him? I've heard the wise affirm there are several qualities required to the making of so great a rarity, including virtue, good looks, health, intelligence, an adequate estate, and a good disposition. But since I'm hardly like to get a spouse with all these qualifications, I desire no more of them than would most conduce to a young woman's happiness.*

A. In the first place, don't be too picky in your choice, lest you should get none at all or the worst that offers, which is the common fate of you critical ladies. Remember that good husbands are like to be scarce.... Then if you have choice to make, choose first one that has piety or at least moral honesty.... Don't give yourself to one of mean parentage, who will probably ... use you ill when he has you.... Nor on the other side dote on that airy name, a gentleman, where there's no perquisites of estate and true honor, much less on a good face.... Nor choose a wit ... or at best he'll be likely to love himself too much to admire you for long. Nor is there any more necessity of his being a scholar.... Much less choose one who has nothing but wealth or everything without it, ... unless you have enough for both, for you'll soon find the bed itself uneasy, if the cradle be full and the cupboard empty.... A good disposition ... does well in a man though more necessary in a woman.... As to the precedence of these qualifications, or the order wherein we think they ought to be desired: 1. virtue. 2. adequate estate. 3. health. 4. a good disposition. 5. good looks. 6. intelligence. [Q.1, 11:19, 12 September 1693]

Q. *I have an equal passion for a virgin and a young widow about the same age, with equal good disposition, beauty, and education. They both love me equally and I may marry either when I wish. The virgin has 500£, the widow 700£. The widow has two children, but they are provided for. I am not in debt and live very well by my profession, but I must marry one of them. I am equally in love with both and don't know which to choose. Pray tell me what would you do, were this your own case, and what would you advise me to? Your opinion shall be the guide to the entire future happiness of the most passionate, distressed, and most confounded lover on earth.*

A. And perhaps you'll be just as wise as before, after our sage advice.... Widows are cunning, but she can't deceive you in one respect.... The widow has 200£ more, but then she has two children. They may be provided for, but they are still her responsibility.... Among all the women's accomplishments, you say nothing about wit. If there's any difference, that decides the case: choose her that has the least. Ten to one, the other will think she has more than you and will take pride in outwitting you. But if they match in mind, estate, wit, disposition, and all, certainly their caresses must differ.... But if that doesn't decide the matter, we can think of only one key difference. Choose her that's shorter, for her clothes will cost less; and if both are the same height, let chance decide. [Q.9, 15:4, 15 September 1694]

Q. *I have for almost four years courted a young gentlewoman who always received me with great respect even before I acquired any inheritance. She at my request refused very good matches. About a year ago I inherited an estate of 400£ per annum left me by a friend. Recently another friend died and left me 200£ per annum more, but on condition that I never would marry the lady in question. If I did, that estate would go to another. Be pleased to understand that the lady is not worth more than 200£. Query: Should I leave the 200£ per annum and take the lady, or leave the lady and take the money?*

A. Never doubt, man, but take the lady. A good wife is worth more than your whole estate. Besides, you can neither in conscience or gratitude forsake her unless you can . . . recompence her for what she has lost at your request. Neither can you dispose of yourself without her consent if any engagements have passed between you, as probably there have been. [Q.6, 15:7, 25 September 1694]

Q. *I am advised by a friend to marry a bankrupt merchant's daughter. She drinks until she is drunk and then lies out all night, but through inheritance from her mother will have four thousand pounds plus a great many jewels that will amount to as much more. Therefore, I would desire your opinion whether it is better for me to marry a gentlewoman of lesser fortune and good reputation rather than the other with all her money and bad qualities. I rely upon your judgments. . . . I know you are friends to the fair sex, and while I live unmarried I am depriving one of them of a very great blessing, for having been acquainted with myself near five and twenty years, I am well assured I have all the necessary qualities of a good husband.*

A. We wish all the fair sex well, and . . . were it in our power we'd find as many men like you pretend to be as would supply all the deserving fair ones. But since at present we have only you to bestow, we are willing to give you to the best, which is to the good woman, although her purse is the lightest. [Q.4, 16:17, 12 February 1695]

Q. *One of my sisters (for whose welfare I am extremely concerned) has a plentiful fortune in my hands. I am willing to entrust it only to a husband with whom she may live happily. She and I differ in the choice of such a man, so I have prevailed upon her to be advised by you. Here is the question (admitting these facts to be true): Two gentlemen have offered themselves. One makes his addresses because of her future prospects, for he has an encumbered estate unworthy of her fortune. The other courts her out of a pure affection, having no need to prey upon her portion because his ample estate well deserves her. The first is skilled in the art of rhetoric and plausible gallantries that engage the minds of the soft sex. The second is honest, modest, downright, and sincere. They are both personable men. Pray let her know which is the most proper object of her affection or more fit to make her a husband. We ask in some pain for your answer, and if it does not come suddenly, she and I may be unhappy.*

A.   We very much doubt that she will be persuaded that you have given us an accurate description of her two suitors. If she believed what you have written, our opinion would not be needed because the qualities of the latter are much to be preferred. Nor would it be improper for her to examine whether his honest, downright sincerity might deserve the name of churlishness, and his money only make him appear to you better than he really is. . . . If you love your sister as you pretend, you must consider which man will make the kindest and most obliging husband as well as which will be the richest. Money alone cannot make us happy, although that mistaken opinion has caused a great many unhappy marriages. Even so, conveniences are desirable when they can be afforded, and to be happy without them requires more resignation than most persons are capable of. [Q.2, 18:9, 13 August 1695]

Q.   *A lady with a good fortune has a mind to marry and dispose of her person and it. But she is unwilling to have a fool, a fop, a beau, a meddler in household affairs, a book-learned sot, or one they call a sober, honest man. I mean by that a man who goes plodding about all day, minding only the main chance. Then in the evening for his diversion he drinks his pint or smokes for some hours in a coffeehouse with company that pleases him, then comes home and grumbles at his wife if the day's expenses have been a half-penny extraordinary. He will buy his wife some good clothes to go abroad with him on holidays or to a neighbor's christening, hardly otherwise allowing her to stir. Sometimes he gives her a crown or half a crown in her pocket, of which she must render an exact account. I say, if a lady has to make her choice, which of these do you think is the least evil? And if she likes none of them, what sort of husband must she choose?*

A. The lady's a little difficult to please, although we confess she seems to have reason. But we can easily tell she's not in haste to be married, if she waits until a man offers who has none of the characteristics she describes.

It's now time to compare these fine rivals one with the other and see which of them best deserves the honor of a lady's love. For the first, a fool, ... time has been when he stood as fair as any, nay, was snapped up by the ladies, and they almost quarreled over who should have him for a husband. But we ... are unwilling to believe ... that many of the fair sex would make choice of him now. ... A wise woman will not and need not desire to have her will more than a wise man would permit her—Exit fool. Now for the fop, ... he has a little wit ... and may make an indifferent plaything but a very bad husband. The beau is only ... a fortune-hunter, and therefore the ladies must look to themselves. ... He's in love with his clothes as much as the fop is with himself. ... As for a household meddler, ... he'll be more troublesome to your maids in the kitchen than to you. ... But a book-learned sot: the truth is that it's very hard to have him always making love to his books and forget his own flesh and blood. It would tempt a lady to wish herself a book ... but for the most part those wives have no great reason to complain. ... Lastly, for the sober, honest man, who minds the main chance, etc., ... Why all this is pretty tolerable.... We suppose the lady means by it a humdrum, soulless, wooden fellow, a mere husband, with no life, nor edge, nor conversation, in a word, a trading blockhead, which no ingenious woman sure would be bound apprentice to for life, if she could avoid it....

However, even this we think much more tolerable than most of his rivals.... This plodding main-chance fellow will secure you good clothes and one of the highest pews in the church while he lives, and if he happens to die, leave... your fortune better than ever. Nor have we forgot him that we left plodding in his study, whom perhaps sympathy makes us inclined to vote for before all the rest. He's no fool, though he looks like one. He's generally sound and honest, so are not fop and beau. He plagues you not in the kitchen ... but lets you alone to rule and order his family, buy as many fine clothes as you will, do what you will. And if you wouldn't have an angel, where would you ever find a better? And so much for this weighty question, on which we have been something long. [*AO*, 2:251–54]

Q. *There is a gentleman whose friends are very desirous to see him settled before their death. He has now the offer of four wives. The first has a very considerable fortune, but nothing else that is praiseworthy to recommend her. This lady he despises, but his friends prefer her. The second is a very beautiful lady, young, gay, and brisk, and though she is not overwise, yet she is very attractive, and he could love her extremely. The third is a lady of great goodness, high generosity, and a world of wit. She he esteems above them all, but knows not how to decide, for there's a fourth that courts him ... who is the veriest coquette in town, yet despite that is every way a desirable match. In these circumstances, your advice as disinterested and impartial persons is earnestly desired.*

Pray give what you'd follow yourselves in the same condition.... Should he comply with his relations by choosing the rich heiress and so advance himself in the world, though he can never

love one so unlovely both in body and mind? Or should his fancy
lead him and he marry that pretty lady, whose person he is so
infinitely taken with, but knows she will never make a suitable
companion? Or should his judgment prevail and he prefer her who
does not have the fortune of the first nor the beauty of the second,
even though she is very agreeable.... He is assured she will make
him not only a good wife but a faithful friend. Or should he be so
generously grateful as to take her that loves him, though he realizes
her daily impertinences will distract him?

A.   Poor gentleman! He's like to be stifled with kisses.... How
many an honest man now would be glad of the worst bit of
his leavings? But to business. If the propagation of money
were the only end of marriage, the first would do best. If
neither men nor women had souls,... the second would be
most desirable. If a man were obliged... only to respond to a
woman's desires, then let him take the last that's in love with
him. But if he's for a match through and through, of body
and soul together, let him have and hold it with the third,
who, if they have but enough between them to live without
contempt or care, can need no fortune, while she has so
large a share of wit, goodness, and generosity. We assure him
this is the course we'd take ourselves and the choice we'd
make, if he has not done it already. For generally those that
are once married (at least for a while) think they've the best
in the world, and every honest husband is bound to believe
so. [*AO*, 3:5]

Querists frequently asked about negotiations and discussions
that preceded marriage, including inquiries about property
issues and the words of the marriage ceremony. Two of the
examples below reveal that the Athenians changed their minds
within a two-month period about whether men should fully
disclose their financial situations to prospective wives before
marriage. Perhaps negative reactions to their first answer can
be inferred.

Q. *When a man is marrying, and says, "with this ring I thee wed," why does he also say, "with my body I thee worship and with all my worldly goods I thee endow," when as soon as they are married, he becomes the head and what was hers is his, and not his hers?*

A. This is a mistake. His worldly goods are as much hers after the marriage, as her own were before marriage. But marriage makes a difference. Whereas before they might each dispose of their own without rendering any account to each other, now in justice they are obliged to each other to dispose of goods by a joint consent.... As for becoming the head, it may very well agree with his promise of worship... in the form of matrimony, being equivalent to a promise of great care and high respect, which the bridegroom promises his bride, whom he is to regard and cherish as his own flesh. [Q.5, 2:21, undated, after 26 July 1691]

Q. *If a single man who is much in debt and can't conveniently live unmarried has a fair offer with a woman of a good fortune by which he might pay all his debts and live comfortably in the world—is he obliged to make her acquainted with his circumstances when he courts her and to run the hazard of not obtaining her?*

A. By no means. Every man should make the best of himself and his fortunes that he honestly can, but he first ought in this case to take a particular care that he hasn't been cheated.... Nor ought he actually to affirm himself worth more than he really is, nor to marry any person without a sufficient fortune to discharge his obligations, ... lest he makes her, himself, and perhaps many others miserable. [Q.7, 3:4, 8 August 1691]

Q. *Would it be greater prudence and honesty for a person of a narrow fortune to conceal his unhappy circumstances until after marriage or to make his mistress acquainted with the same as soon as he has gained her affections?*

A. We should think it the most prudent and most handsome way to reveal it to her before marriage, for a woman of sense will rather be pleased than otherwise that she can make the fortunes of a gentleman.... But she might resent it very ill if a cheat should be put upon her, when she once comes to know it. [Q7, 4:3, 6 October 1691]

Q. *I have wooed a maid, and have got her consent to marry me, but she refuses to consummate the marriage unless I will agree to omit those words in the service that oblige her to honor and obey her husband. However, she is willing to accept your judgment in the matter. Pray be so kind as to answer without delay.*

A. If she expects one dispensation it is but fair you should have another.... If she leaves out [honor and obey] you should have liberty to omit [with my body I thee worship], and then we think things will be pretty even. If she does not agree to this, we will and decree that you shall not agree to the other. [Q5, 10:14, 13 May 1693]

Q. *A friend of mine was courted by a gentleman... continually pursuing her whether in town or country, making his addresses as well by friends as himself. She was averse to his suit a long time ... but she could perceive nothing disorderly about his temper or actions and began to think she would be extremely happy in a husband. She being still importuned by him, promised to have him.... Soon all things were prepared for the wedding, but a day or two before he told her that marriage was only a political institution and that before God they were man and wife already. Therefore, he thought it a needless ceremony and could never approve it. At that, she was very much startled and went out of the room. She left him and has since neither heard from nor seen him. She now wishes to be satisfied whether she may lawfully marry another man notwithstanding her previous promise, for she has met a gentleman that's very agreeable.*

A. She's undoubtedly free to marry whom she pleases, for she did not promise to have him whether he would or no, and since he has refused her, she's anybody's that can catch her. [Q.5, II:17, 5 September 1693]

Q. *One that is in their Majesties' service, yet in a small station and with no hopes of being promoted, desires your advice in the following difficulty. A woman has a considerable quantity of money, so if he can really love her person as well as her money, she would . . . disburse one half of her estate. If she could obtain his discharge, she would furnish him with all things necessary. . . . He has considered her offer but with all her money he cannot love her. Therefore, he desires your advice whether he should leave their Majesties' service, in which he is greatly inclined to continue though in a very small post, or take himself to that woman with all her money?*

A. It's hardly honest to quit so glorious a service when there's so much need of more men to engage in it. It's absolutely dishonest to take anybody's money without giving them some valuable consideration. It's true, there's body for body, but without the heart that's but a very dull business. On the whole, it's plain that you ought not to sell yourself to this kind woman, let her bid ever so high for you, unless you can make a fair bargain of it, which you yourself say you cannot. [Q.1, II:28, 14 October 1693]

Q. *Is it lawful to marry a gentlewoman who has not been christened, for her parents are Anabaptists (though she is not)? The gentleman has resolved that if he does marry her to christen her afterward. He will not proceed until you answer publicly.*

A. We are expressly enjoined not to be unequally yoked with unbelievers; therefore . . . she must show herself an actual believer before marriage by first engaging herself in the profession of Christianity by baptism. [Q.7{8}, 14:7, 12 June 1694]

Q. *I am acquainted with a hectoring gentlewoman who looks down
on a man as a giant would a dwarf. She strongly argues that no
obedience is due from the wife to the husband. She's not married,
but she has taught others what without a doubt she would practice
herself, to say at that solemn covenant of marriage, instead of
honor and obey, honor and no obey. Some have done that through
her enticement. Your judgment of such a person and such a practice
is desired. Perhaps you may convince the gentlewoman otherwise
and prevent others from taking her pernicious counsel.*

A. The ladies must excuse us if for once we here stand up for
men's prerogative, since they cannot deny that we have hith-
erto been as favorable to their liberties and properties as
possible. . . . Power is a delicious morsel, and few that get it
between their teeth have moderation enough to give it up.
Letting this lady marry would have dangerous consequences,
for ten to one she'd propagate that most wicked heresy of
the old Amazons, that it's lawful for wives to swaddle their
husbands. . . . It's therefore the unanimous vote of our society
that neither she nor any of her proselytes and acquaintances
be ever permitted matrimony lest they should subvert the
very order of nature. [Q3, 14:15, 10 July 1694]

Q. *I am a young man lately set up in business. I have but a small stock,
only a few friends, and but little trading, yet I am greatly inclined
to marry. At the same time, I don't well know how to maintain
a wife. I am continually perplexed with unruly desires, by which
I am afraid I'm displeasing God. Although I do what I can to divert
these thoughts, I find them still very powerful, and surely in time
I may be tempted to go beyond the thoughts alone. . . . What must
I do in this case?*

A. We may give you a great deal of good advice and bid you
avoid temptations, fast and pray, etc. But that has not always
been found powerful enough to cast out this devil. . . . If
you can find sufficient means, it will be much the best for

you. Even if not, you must marry with all convenient haste. Perhaps you may get a wife who can add so much to your stock that it may put you in a better way of living, but if you can't do that, you must get one who will help by her own industry or at least be content with your circumstances, whatever they may be. We have several querists facing the same unhappy circumstances, whom we refer to this answer. [Q.1, 18:14, 31 August 1695]

Q.   *I am an apprentice and will have considerable means to set myself up when I finish my service. But currently my friends allow me only a very little spending money, so I owe a young man forty or fifty shillings. He asks me constantly for it and threatens to persecute me until I pay him, but I have asked a young maid I know to lend me that amount. She will not do so unless I marry her. But if I marry her, I shall disoblige my friends, for they have provided a very great fortune for me after my service is complete. I dare not ask them for the money now. Your advice is humbly craved: Should I marry and get this money to prevent further problems? Or how else should I proceed? I am resolved to follow your advice.*

A.   From your question we judge you're hardly worth her money or our answer. But lest your father should lose all his hopes of such a cowardly son, we'll lend our advice if that will do to keep you in the right way. If you have any particular friend to assist you in this matter, your best way is to borrow the money from them. If not and the debtor is still impatient, you may let him know that it's better to have a little patience than never to have the money. It's gratitude and not the law that will force you to pay him, for he can't recover anything that is loaned to anyone underage. Yet if he continues troublesome and you fear he will tell your friends, it's better for you to tell them yourself. They will more likely sooner forgive you for the debt than they would your marrying without their consent. [Q.1, 18:8, 10 August 1695]

Q. *A young apprentice who has served about half his time has a very good opportunity to make an advantageous marriage. Would you advise him to take the opportunity or to let her go and say he cannot marry because he is an apprentice? Gentlemen, pray favor me with a speedy answer.*

A. Fair and gently, lad! Marriage is no football play. If you began your apprenticeship at twenty and have your friends' consent, we give you permission to marry. But if you started at the younger more common age our answer differs.... Not one marriage in five hundred made before the age of twenty-five or thereabouts proves happy. The boy loves a wife that the man has reason to dislike.... Therefore, we believe if you'll follow our advice and not marry until you are older and wiser, you'll some years from now think yourself much obliged to us for the advice. [Q.4, 19:7, 19 November 1695]

CHAPTER 3

"Read History (Nothing Amorous)"

PARENTAL CONSENT

PROPOSED MARRIAGES WERE SUPPOSED to be approved by parents or guardians. Most queries about parental consent came from young people who disagreed with their parents over the choice of a spouse, either because the parents had prohibited a particular marriage or because they promoted unions with partners their sons or daughters did not prefer. On the positive side, though, parents could extricate children from difficult situations by refusing consent to marriages no longer desired.

Many of the questions about consent revolved around considerations of property and inheritance. Although letter writers never specified how much money was at issue in these intrafamilial disputes, the content of their questions suggests that this group of querists was better off financially than those who wrote to the Athenians on other topics. Even though the published responses frequently criticized the rash behavior of courting couples, the Athenians also expressed sympathy for correspondents' problems with their parents or other relatives.

Q. *Is it convenient for a lady to marry one for whom she has an aversion in obedience to her parents?*

A. We answer it's by no means so. Parents are not to dispose of their children like cattle, nor to make them miserable because they happened to give them being. Parents are indeed generally granted a negative voice. But that would perhaps not hold if they were unreasonable, if they have given permission before, or if after an engagement too deep to be broken, they endeavor to retract it. That parents have a despotic positive vote none ... will pretend. [Q.13, 1:13, 5 May 1691]

Q. *A certain bully of the town has by his cunning instigations drawn in a young lady of a considerable fortune into a solemn contract and vow of marriage ... without the consent of the lady's parents. Query: Is it in the power of the parents (the lady also consenting) to make void that contract?*

A. We don't say that parents have that right over their children as to marry them against their own consent, ... yet we affirm that children cannot dispose of themselves without the consent of their parents.... So that our answer is that it lies in the parents' power to vacate the abovementioned contract, ... but she cannot do it herself. [Q.3, 3:16, 29 August 1691]

Q. *Is it permissible for a good man to marry his daughter to one of a vicious life but with a good estate, rather than an honest one with a smaller fortune?*

A. If it is permissible, we think it neither kind nor prudent for him to do so, since his daughter is likely to be unhappier with the rich ill man than with the other not in so good circumstances, if truly pious and religious. [Q.8{9}, 4:13, 10 November 1691]

Q. *A young man is attracted to a young woman and wishes to acquaint her parents with it before he makes any addresses to her. His mother depends on him for maintenance, and the parents of the young woman are so covetous that he thinks they would not consent to the marriage if he tells them about his responsibility for his mother. He desires your judgment if he is bound in conscience or honesty to acquaint them with it.*

A. We can't see that he has any obligation to acquaint the parents with that circumstance, though neither ought he to deny it if they ask and he can't avoid an answer. But after he has made any progress in his courtship, or at least before marriage, he should let the young woman know about this responsibility to prevent many problems that might hereafter follow his present silence. If this expression of duty to a parent should make her break off the courtship, he is better to be without her than have her. [Q5, 13:17, 3 April 1694]

Q. *A friend of mine with a very good trade is passionately in love with a notorious capricious and faithless woman of the town.... I fear besides spoiling his trade and ruining his fortune she will persuade him to marry her. Query: Should I in conscience and friendship acquaint his father and the rest of his relations about this situation before it is too late?*

A. To convince the young man of his folly, obtain accounts from several people of her public lewdness. Point out that by keeping her company he will ruin his reputation and spoil his fortune. Also, that if he married her he would probably find it very hard if not impossible to make her an honest woman.... If this or the like methods won't do, you ought to acquaint his father before it's too late. [Q5, 13:20, 14 April 1694]

Q. *With grief and deep concern I renew my request to you. You have been often and earnestly solicited to resolve a question sent by a young lady who unfortunately contracted herself some time ago in the most solemn manner to a gentleman contrary to the wishes of her parents. She now recognizes her fault and is willing to comply with them by marrying another. But the first man refuses to release her, which has created the question for you. Can she without the consent of the first comply with her parents and marry the second man? The thing is real and the lady is greatly troubled, so your speedy resolution of the point is humbly desired.*

A. If the parents disallowed the first engagement as soon as they heard of it, it was in their power to make it void, but if they knew about it and continued silent, that was a tacit consent. They cannot afterward honorably or honestly reverse that consent. Parents should comply with the inclinations of their children unless such a marriage would ruin them. It's the children who must be happy or miserable because of the choice of a spouse.... We daily see many bad consequences of forced matches. [Q7, 16:17, 12 February 1695]

Q. *A sixteen-year-old lady we know has been forced by her mother to marry a twelve-year-old fool, because the mother had an ardent desire to marry the boy's father, and he would not agree to marry her unless her daughter married his son.... Now I desire to know your opinion about the match, and further whether the daughter may not divorce the boy, for they never bedded together more than two hours.... You may think it strange that the daughter's other relations have not intervened, but they know that if this fool has no children they will get more than 500£ a year, and so they hold their tongues. Even though I say the lady is sixteen, when she was married she was only fourteen and the lad was ten.*

A. Unless she is very prudent, the young lady may suffer all her life for this uncaring and unjust act of her mother. But because the wedding and bedding are wholly past and irrecoverably confirmed, her happiness and duty requires her to be satisfied. Her true friends will endeavor to make her easy and contented with her marriage. [Q7, 18:21, 24 September 1695]

Sometimes parents or guardians flatly refused to agree to a son's or daughter's marriage.

Q. *I love a young lady so much that, though I frequent the park and the playhouse, I cannot meet there anyone whom I can find nearly*

as handsome. Her charms have absolutely possessed my heart;
I cannot begin to love another. . . . But my friends won't let me
marry her. What shall I do to divert myself and make the time
seem shorter till I can marry her? I would join the army, but my
relations deny me that too. If you will, gentlemen, instruct me by
a speedy answer.

A. Poor man, will no new face cure you? . . . If you are willing
to follow the wise advice of your friends (for they know
the world better than you) and will endeavor to disengage
yourself from the young lady, travel, if that is permitted by
your relations. Observe all the curiosities you meet with,
but if your affairs won't permit that, study at first history,
which is diverting, and then follow as your interests direct
you. By all means avoid idleness and the sight of the lady or
anything that may remind you of her. Find some agreeable
ingenious acquaintances who have conquered cupid and
know how to value their freedom. If you follow this method,
a little time will infallibly recover you. [Q.6, 6:26, 26 March
1692]

Q. *I've obtained the love of a young lady of considerable fortune who*
is only fifteen years old and whose relations are all dead except
one who is her guardian. He has the management of all her estate.
Query: May she lawfully marry without her guardian's knowledge
or consent?

A. The law having entrusted the infant to the guardian's care
and . . . he being her only living relation, we must conclude
that she can't either prudently or lawfully dispose of herself
without his consent and knowledge. We are aware we shall
unavoidably disoblige all the fortune hunters in town by
this statement. But the case is altered if the lady is twenty-one, if her guardian treats her badly at present or plans to
cheat her in the future . . . or hopes to reserve her for some
blockhead of his own begetting. . . . In these circumstances,
if a gentleman really deserving her should offer, nay if such

a one lacks only a fortune and the lady has enough for both, we think she does not err if she chooses a more careful and intimate guardian than him her parents left her. [Q5, 7:19, 31 May 1692]

Q. *I have heard a young lady make such lamentation for want of a husband that would grieve a heart of marble. She has neither father nor mother, but lives with an old miserly uncle, who will not permit any to court the poor creature, hoping in a little time to make himself master of her fortune, which is very considerable. She is to be disposed of as her uncle thinks fit or else not to have one farthing. This poor husbandless young creature would be extremely obliged to you for your advice and direction.*

A. Either this poor compassionable lady must try if she can find any romantic knight of a good fortune, who … will take her for better or worse, without the encumbrance of a fortune. Or else they must try to be too cunning for the old fellow and trick him into a consent. Or she must patiently … live as merry as she can in her sad circumstances, for it is possible she may outlive her good uncle and possess his estate instead of his swallowing hers. [Q.2, 8:11, 4 October 1692]

Q. *I presumed some time since to crave your advice in a case that almost distracts me. . . . I am the most miserable creature in the whole world. My parents still continue so cruel as daily to command me not to act on my love. Nay, they plainly tell me that if I do they will never look upon me more. Yet I fear if I cannot marry him, I must die for it. Dear gentlemen, pity me, and … let me know your thoughts what course is best to take.*

A. The best method we know of, is this, if your own entreaties won't prevail, make use of the interest of some of your friends. . . . Avoid solitariness, read history (nothing amorous), use much company (only that which is innocent), and never indulge yourself to think of your passion when alone. And what is yet the best remedy, be frequent in your devotions and beg a quiet, peaceful mind. And this method can't fail. [Q.4, 9:25, 7 March 1693]

Q. *It was my unhappy fortune to be courted by a gentleman that all my friends are extremely against. They sent me away from him, thinking that absence might part our affections. But it had no such effect upon either of us, but the contrary upon me.... Now this person is come to the place where I am and renews the same thing again. I cannot withstand him.... Gentlemen, give me your advice, whether in conscience I may marry this man without sinning against God or disobeying my parents, for they are still against it. I am willing to obey them, but how might I gain their consent if possible?*

A. You ought not, nor can you in conscience, surrender without their consent.... Yet if the gentleman is really a deserving and suitable match, or if he lacks only an equal fortune to yours and has enough comfortably to maintain you, we'll tell you the most likely way to work upon them. Go to your mother first (if she loves you best, as is usual), fall upon your knees, shed tears plentifully (they'll cost you nothing but a little wringing and a few hard faces), and tell her you can be happy with no other person. Add that although you'll not marry him against your parents' consent, you are resolved never to marry anyone else. You can entreat her, as she ever knew love herself, to pity yours. If you once melt her, let her alone with your father. This way, if any, is like to prevail, and may probably obtain you their consent to make yourself miserable. [Q.3, 11:2, 15 July 1693]

Q. *It was my misfortune to be privately courted by a gentleman of suitable years and quality to mine. I thought him a fit person to be my husband, but our fathers unfortunately disagreed about the match. At that, the young gentleman unknown to his father took a rash resolution to go for Flanders.... To prevent that and to bring him back, in hopes he would be better advised by his friends, I sent him a letter in which I made a solemn promise to marry him even*

without my parents' consent....At his return he very much insists
on that promise, charging me with injustice if I fail to comply.
The query is (since I cannot obtain my parents' consent): Am I in
conscience more obliged to observe the promise or observe the duty
to my parents?

A. You are under the same unhappy circumstance as many oth-
    ers. You have no power to make any vow. Harsh parents
    may annul it as soon as they know it, for you are theirs.
    They have a right to break all contracts made without their
    consent. We think it's very unkind and unreasonable, too,
    when they do it without very just cause, for it is their duty
    to do all things for the felicity and satisfaction of their chil-
    dren as much as is possible. Therefore, all you can do is to
    endeavor to gain their permission, assuring the gentleman
    you'll do your utmost to procure it. [Q.1, 13:13{12}, 17 March
    1694] [*AO*, 2:59]

Q. *I've had the happiness to be well received by a young lady whose*
    estate is far above mine. But her friends are very angry with us.
    May I lawfully marry her without their consent?

A. If either of her parents are living, you cannot lawfully do it.
    If only more distant relations are concerned, the case dif-
    fers. Still, probably her wisest way would be to take their
    advice and leave you to seek another mistress. [Q.5, 15:4, 15
    September 1694]

Q. *I have courted a young gentlewoman for some years and have at last*
    gained her love unknown to either of our parents. If they learned
    of our intrigue, they'd certainly prevent it. If we should marry
    without their consent, we would be disowned and ruined. We know
    it would be in vain to ask their permission. If I talk of leaving her,
    she cries that she will be undone. Pray, what should we do in this
    perplexing condition?

A. Poor fellow! ...You have run yourself into inextricable diffi-
    culties and you cry to Athens for help, but we can only give

you small comfort. . . . All you can do now is to try to use what power you or your friends have over your parents. If they still continue obstinate, you should stay true to one another until the old folks change their minds or die. [Q.6, 15:24, 24 November 1694]

Q. *I make bold to trouble you with the following case: A gentlewoman and myself have passionately loved each other for a considerable time. But both our parents were averse to it and obliged us to promise them never to speak to one another of love again. Yet notwithstanding our promise to them we have continued our passion. I promised before heaven to marry her if she would consent, which she readily did. . . . Now our parents, thinking all was broke off between us, have provided matches for us. She has refused hers, saying she would never marry because of her love for me. But she that my parents have provided for me is so far above the other in beauty, fortune, and all other endowments that I would like to break my engagement. Now pray inform me if my promise to her is inviolable, since it was done without the consent of our parents. May I lawfully marry the other?*

A. You rash and inconstant sparks deservedly bring men's fidelity into ill repute among the ladies. Your parents could prevent your marrying, but why must you be in such haste to marry now? Because she's handsomer—so much the more likely to cuckold you—and she's richer too. . . . With such motives, what does a little whining, trifling constancy and love mean? . . . Still, if your mistress will release you (indeed we think you are not worthy of her), you are free to marry anyone who will accept you. But if she doesn't release you, you can neither honorably nor innocently leave her. [Q.5, 16:19, 19 February 1695]

Sometimes parents pressed children to accept spouses the children wanted to reject, and the Athenians counseled against marriage for the time being.

Q. *A gentlewoman aged eighteen with a tolerable fortune has been courted by a fifty-eight-year-old man who has been very well received by her parents. She displeased her parents by at first rejecting the suit, but her relations have argued that there is a great scarcity of good husbands these days. That argument and the hope for a good estate seem to have convinced her to like her old spark. It's impossible to tell, but it's thought her duty to her parents has influenced her in this affair. I do not criticize the old gentleman other than for his gray hairs, but desire that you would answer the following questions:*

1. *How far does the duty of a child oblige her to comply with her parents in such a case?*
2. *If the young lady should not heartily feel affection for her spark, can a person of his age win her affections better after marriage than before?*
3. *Is it possible for a young woman to love such a person sufficiently to make her life happy hereafter?*

A.1. She must not obstinately refuse the advice of her parents, although on the other side they have no power to force her contrary to her own inclinations.

A.2. Matrimony too often proves an antidote rather than an inducement to love. This is a dangerous case. Ten to one, love never appears after marriage, especially where there's such a disparity of years.

A.3. Some outcomes are improbable but not impossible, and this marriage may justly fit in that category. Still, such unequal matches are very imprudent and they should be avoided by all wise persons. [Q.1, 14:2, 26 May 1694]

Q. *A well-bred young lady from a good family with a moderate fortune and a free and airy temperament has been courted by an elderly man. He was formerly a libertine and is both morose and jealous but is very rich. By the persuasion and solicitous desires of her father and other relations, she has promised to marry him. The same young lady has likewise been courted by a young gentleman from a good family. He is well educated with a suitable fortune, sober conversation, and an agreeable temperament, but is at present unemployed. To please her father and other friends she has rejected his suit, but at the same time it's believed she would be happier with him than with the old spark. As you are persons unconcerned in the matter, your advice is desired. What is most proper for the young lady to do in this affair? . . . She is well satisfied the young gentleman loves her and he would marry her without a portion.*

A.   We are certain we won't please you, because our advice is for the lady to marry neither of them. Not the younger, because that would be against the consent of her parents, nor the elder, because his temperament is so disagreeable. . . . Nor can her parents force her to any such match, for it is just to allow children a negative voice in those matters. . . . She should not marry one for whom she reasonably has so great an aversion. [Q.2, 14:11, 26 June 1694]

Q.   *Gentlemen, I desire your help. There is a very old-old woman who says that she's mightily in love with me. She has an estate of a hundred pounds a year but is a confounded heavy brandy drinker. My father earnestly wishes me to marry her, but I can't endure the sight of her. I'm very young, but for all that I am in love with a young woman about my own age. She has only a little money, but she's a special good housewife, can get her living herself, and is willing to have me, but my father is vehemently against it because this old drunkard has got so much money. Pray give me your advice what a poor young fellow ought to do in this miserable case and you'll extremely oblige me.*

A.   What should you do? Tarry until you're older. You should be wiser before you marry and ruin a woman who has no more than yourself, unless your father consents and you can support yourself as well as she. As for the old woman, your father does not have the power to make you marry her by the laws of either God or man. . . . Your duty is to refuse what your father orders as handsomely and dutifully as you can. [Q.1, 15:3, 11 September 1694]

More often than sons, daughters seem to have encountered a particular dilemma: they preferred one suitor and their parents another, often an older or wealthier man whom the young woman did not love. But one son also wrote to seek the Athenians' advice.

Q.   *I've promised marriage against the consent of my friends. Suspecting this, they have forbid my lover to make any further addresses and commanded me not to entertain him any longer. Further, they resolve to marry me to another man, for whom I have a great aversion. Your direction is desired: How shall I behave myself in this difficult affair?*

A.1. If the person be of years of discretion, we think a promise to marry is binding, although not lawfully made.... We think the lack of parental consent is a very just obstruction as long as they live, but not longer.... So far then as children are under parental control, they undoubtedly sin in making any such promises and cannot perform them until their parents consent or die, thereby freeing them....

A.2. Children are neither livestock nor slaves. We think they have therefore at least a negative voice even where there was no prior obligation and much more where there is.... To sum up: the positive promise here was unlawful, nor is it to be actually performed without the parents' consent or death, yet the parent has no power to vacate this promise, much less to force their child to marry any other. [Q.3, 7:9, 26 April 1692]

Q.   *I am a young woman that has been very dutiful to my parents, ... but now they have proposed a match for me whom I cannot love. Therefore, I humbly desire your advice: How shall I discharge my duty? Shall I oblige my parents and live an uncomfortable life ... or*

disoblige them by refusing what they so earnestly importune me to?
This is a real matter of fact, therefore I desire your speedy answer.

A.   As a child can't lawfully dispose of itself without the consent of its parents, so on the other side, we don't understand that the parents can marry their children without their consent.... We think the many unhappy examples of such matches should prevail with parents. We think children are not undutiful if they deny their compliance. [Q.5, 9:25, 7 March 1693]

Q.   *I am courted by two gentlemen. The one I have been acquainted with from my childhood and never knew him to be extravagant.... His profession is honorable and our fortunes equal, besides I believe he entirely loves me. Our friends on both sides were very well satisfied with the match till the second lover came. He is a perfect country squire, whose conversation has been wholly amongst his dogs or company as brutish, ... but he's blessed with a far larger estate than the former. That has influenced my father so as to order me to discharge my former lover. Your advice is desired in this matter.*

A.   Our general advice is to consider that the fear of God and a good temperament are more happy qualifications in so near a consort than abundance of wealth.... All we can say is that you may not act contrary to your father's pleasure in disposing of yourself, nor can he by any right of nature force you to marry whoever he pleases.... Parents are more often in the right than their children, and ... you ought to weigh your parent's reasons well and consult with others that are wise and pious.... You must ... consider always that these things are but for a while. All the most material trials and circumstances of this life entitle us to be no more than actors or probationers for the life to come. [Q.1, 10:25, 20 June 1693]

Q.   *My father had two sons, my elder brother and myself. He had a plentiful estate in land for my brother, but my fortune was not great,*

I being bred to the law. Near us lived a young lady of surpassing beauty and great wit and a fortune (exceeding what I could expect as a younger brother) entirely at her own disposal, her friends being dead. To her my father commanded me to make addresses of love, which I did and got her goodwill. We were engaged each to other as surely as vows and promises could make us.... My father was well pleased, but since then my elder brother has died. I'm left the only son and heir. Now my father forbids me to prosecute my suit any further, thinking I may have a greater fortune. If I do not desist, he threatens to deny me his blessing, though his estate is entailed so that he cannot dispose of it from me after his death. I have solemnly promised to marry this young woman and the day is appointed. Pray, your direction in this matter.

A. Disobedience is as much your duty in the present case as it would be if your father should command you to kill your friend or betray your country. His first command has precluded his second. [Q5, II:II, 15 August 1693]

Q. *A young lady who will have a very considerable fortune has for some years been courted by a gentleman of a very good estate, who was not only approved by her father but entertained and mightily encouraged. He advised and persuaded his daughter to accept the suitor, but now that she begins to favor him, the old gentleman, having got a prospect of a better match, forbids him his daughter's company. He directs her not to entertain the young man until he sees how affairs will go elsewhere. If those don't work out, they may continue and proceed to matrimony as soon as they please. Now, gentlemen, your opinion is desired in this matter and your advice to the young lady. How far is she obliged to comply with her father and how should she behave herself with the aforesaid gentleman?*

A. She having engaged herself by her father's consent, neither the father nor daughter had power to quit the obligations without the gentleman's consent or some other just cause.... The estate should have been considered before and is not now a sufficient cause for an honest man to break a child's engagement, especially when she had her father's approval.... She ought to finish what she has begun. [Q.5, 14:17, 17 July 1694] [*AO*, 2:95]

Q. *About two years ago I was courted by a young man who gained my affections. We decided to be married, upon which we broke a piece of money. He made a vow to me and I one to him. I was then about 16 years old. We did this contrary to the knowledge of my father and mother, who hated him. About a month ago another young man came to court me with the consent of my parents, but I was troubled by his presence because my affections were fixed on the former suitor. My father and mother examined me strictly, and I told them the whole story. My parents immediately vowed never to see me any more or to take any further care of me. But with the assistance of good friends, I have now reconciled with them on condition that I never marry the first or ever keep him company. I have nothing but what my parents will be pleased to give me, but the first suitor does not care about that.*

Gentlemen, I humbly beg your speedy answer as to how far the duty of a child lies to careful parents in regard to marriage. If I should be forced by my father and mother to marry the latter man, may I do it lawfully, although I have told him and them I never can love him? I would willingly act with a good conscience in this affair and shall altogether do as you advise. I believe the first young man is as able as the last to maintain me.

A. Children are at their parents' disposal and cannot contract any vows without their consent.... Much of a child's happiness depends on the choice of a spouse, and it's they who must suffer if they are unequally matched. It's probable your father and mother love you and some consideration of that affection could convince them to consider your own inclinations.... If they persist in refusing their consent to the first, you'll do very well to likewise refuse to marry the last. We advise none to marry but where they can love. Life is either agreeable or disagreeable according to the share there is of love, and it is very seldom observed to come after marriage. [Q.4, 14:25, 14 August 1694]

Q. *A gentleman whom I like with six hundred a year courts me. I am also being courted by a gentleman with three thousand a year, but he is very unsuitable for me in both age and temperament. The qualities of the first please me and the estate of the last tempts my friends. I beg your advice what to do.*

A. Ten thousand a year won't compensate for gray hairs and ill humor. Therefore, you'd best live unmarried until you can win your friends' consent to the former. If in the meantime you are unhappy, at least you'll avoid being miserable. [Q.4, 15:5, 18 September 1694]

In one case, the man's parents disagreed with the woman's. When he followed their advice, the Athenians criticized him.

Q. *A gentleman making his address to a young woman was well received both by her and her parents. On her desire he promised her marriage if her parents would consent to it . . . and he made her an absolute promise. At length, the young gentlewoman was sent to a boarding school. Not long after the gentleman began to treat with her parents concerning her fortune. They would not . . . consent that she should marry him till after a considerable time had passed. . . . His circumstances were such that if he waited as long as they wished, he was in danger of financial ruin. At the same time, the gentleman had an offer of a larger fortune and wrote to his parents concerning it. . . . They advised him to quit the former and embrace the offer of the latter, which he accordingly did and married her. . . . The question is: Did he err in marrying the second when he had so absolutely promised the first? He is now exceedingly troubled and desires your judgment concerning his action and directions how he should now behave himself.*

A. There are general rules of prudence, truth, and justice, all which the gentleman seems to have broken. . . . He did not do well in beginning a business of that importance without his parents' permission. He did yet worse in making such an absolute promise.... It looks suspicious that the weightiest motive for the gentleman changing his affections was that he thought his second mistress had a better fortune than the former. The only thing that can almost excuse him is that he was in danger of ruin had he remained unmarried for long. But the question still is: How great was that danger?... It might have excused him had he tried but failed to obtain the hand of the first.... All the gentleman can do in the present case is to ask God pardon for his disobedience, rashness, and unfaithfulness, and the injured persons for his inconstancy and falsehood. But not further we think to disturb his mind or make his life uneasy. Sure enough, this marriage holds good, now it's done, though we think he ought not to have done it. [Q3, 15:20, 10 November 1694] [*AO*, 2:467–68]

Under some circumstances, the Athenians decided that couples did not need consent from parents or relatives in order to marry.

Q. *A gentlewoman is at years of discretion and has been educated at a great distance from her relations, who always left her to her own management. After an honorable courtship made and an equal return expressed and confirmed by vows, can the rules of duty free her from the engagement solemnly contracted?*

A. The meaning of the question, I suppose, is whether in the case thus stated, a parent's disallowing such vows or contracts does really annul them or not.... We can by no means... approve the power of the father to annul any such vow. [Q3, 1:18, 23 May 1691]

Q. *I have long been acquainted with a gentlewoman, a widow, who has an excellent temperament. That more than the property she*

possesses led me to court her. She gave me an absolute promise
of marriage. However, we find much opposition from her friends,
which seems only . . . to be my lack of an estate. At first they did
not seem to oppose our match but rather accepted it until a rival
appeared with a considerable estate. I can honestly say that he
has not ingenuity enough to keep him from the contempt of his
neighbors. The widow's friends have endeavored by wrongfully
impairing my reputation to persuade her to dislike me, but I proved
my innocence of their charges. Nothing can now discourage her
from carrying out the vow she made me except for her friends'
dislike of the match. We beg your advice. Shouldn't we better marry
now than fulfill a pledge we made to live single until her friends
die, because she lives altogether independent of them?

A. There's not the least reason why you should oblige her covetous friends, who in this case can pretend to no power over
her. If you'll take our advice, get a license and be married
tomorrow, which will effectually decide the controversy.
[Q.1, 14:15, 10 July 1694]

Q. *I am an old maid, which, you'll say, is not too common. I have out-*
lived many good offers of marriage, but now a gentleman I like
offers himself and I know he loves me well. His circumstances in
the world are also good. My parents are dead, but my remaining
relations are against the match, though I don't know why. . . . I
have no person to advise me, and therefore beg you would direct
me what to do.

A. First, you should consider whether your friends have any sufficient reason to oppose the match. You owe them no more
than the possibility of taking their advice. If they remain
refractory without any cause and you love each other, go
ahead and marry to end the dispute. [Q.6, 15:1, 4 September
1694]

Q. *Friends of mine, a man and woman, have contracted mutual*
love to each other and are near the point of marriage. He is an

artist, a person of very good business, reputation, and honesty, and able enough to maintain his mistress if occasion requires. . . . The woman is a virtuous, intelligent person and newly set up in the world, partly with money and the rest with her credit. They love one another very well, but the woman's mother, on whom the daughter does not depend financially, will not consent. . . . So the young woman is torn between duty and love and very much troubled.

A.   Her being independent of her mother frees her to some extent from those strong obligations children generally have to their parents. She is almost as much at her own disposal as a widow is. Yet she ought to think about whether her mother has more reason to be averse to the match than the daughter's passion will let her perceive at first sight. If the mother's attitude is based only on prejudice, she must still do what she can to convince her of that and at least wait some time before marriage. [Q.5, 17:24, 23 June 1695]

Q.   *I am an elderly man with several children. . . . I have one that was a widower for many years with whom I and the rest of my family lived as boarders for some years past. He decided he would marry again, and without my consent or knowledge he courted a woman with only a small estate. I think he ought to have looked higher and not to have damaged the family property. Before that marriage was consummated I forbid it and would have prevented it. . . . But he told me he did not have to ask my consent, for after one marriage he was now his own man . . . and that she was a discreet, sober, honest, and religious woman. . . . So like an undutiful child he left us a year or two ago to make do on our own, whereas we might have lived comfortably together. . . . I understand that his wife and he go every month to take communion. . . . I desire first to know if he can be a worthy receiver of the sacrament? . . . Second, if . . . he ought to have sought my consent for his second choice or not?*

A. Your son ought in prudence to have asked your advice and consent. If you had refused him, he should have waited some time before remarrying out of respect for you. But we think he was at his own liberty.... It now lies upon you ... not to be bitter against your son. You must be reconciled to him. [Q.1, 17:26, 29 June 1695]

CHAPTER 4

"*A Contract Solemnly Made*"

PROMISES AND VOWS

IN THE ABSENCE OF a legal definition of marriage in England prior to 1753, key questions arose about contracts and promises made by courting couples. Did such contracts constitute the equivalent of marriage? Could they be voided voluntarily by one or both partners? Correspondents wanted to know the answer to that and many other questions about sworn promises to marry, which seem to have been common. But unless querists explicitly described to the Athenians the nature of the vows they mentioned, it is impossible to know whether the vows were made only to themselves, to a prospective partner, or perhaps to God. Some couples broke coins between them to underscore a contract to marry.

The earliest response of the Athenians to a question about engagements was that promises to marry were binding for the duration of the participants' lives, but later answers were more nuanced and even inconsistent, which was unsurprising given the complex circumstances correspondents described. Still, in most cases the Athenians stressed the need for mutual consent if the members of a couple were to go their separate ways. If such consent could not be obtained, the Athenians judged that marriage promises could remain obligatory.

Q. *May a contract solemnly made with all the most sacred invocations be violated by any unfortunate accident or error in life or manners? ...*

And may the offended party abandon the other for a new lover without a joint consent, or whether it may be done with consent?

A. Such a marriage is valid and not to be canceled either with or without the consent of either or both parties, ... for marriage is like a deed of gift—there's no recalling it when once done. So that young persons (for it's too common a vice of the age) should be careful to act no farther than they are willing to stand by. That marriage is not generally what it is taken to be is manifest by the several customs of nations. Those public solemnizations are only for the satisfaction of the world, to avoid scandal and make proper objects for the law to work on in the cases of children, debts, mortgages, and to prevent other persons from intruding. [Q.8, 3:6, 15 August 1691]

Q. *After promises made between two persons, may they lawfully leave each other and accept to court others by mutual consent?*

A. We think they may, the obligation being mutual and just as much on one side as the other. If both give up their part there's no wrong done—Nay, we think it would be very requisite they should do so in some cases. [Q.7, 5:13, 12 January 1692]

Q. *I promised marriage to a young lady. Not long after our engagement, my circumstances required me to travel. . . . She at that time gave as great testimonies of her fidelity as I could desire, but it was not long before she entertained another gentleman. So successful was my rival that doubtless he would have married her, but the plan was revealed the very night before it was to have been put into execution. All their measures were irrecoverably abandoned, her relations being bitterly averse thereto. . . . I have procured a discharge in writing in which we mutually and voluntarily acquit each other from all obligations whatsoever relating to matrimony. . . . Resolve for me whether my unhappy contract is void or how far it obliges me.*

A. Void, Yes. We should be very unhappy creatures if our vows must be in force whether the women are constant or no, for they have their share of fickleness as well as we. [Q.1, 12:20, 30 December 1693]

Q. *A. B. contracted to H. H. and they broke a piece of silver together. They wished that that piece of silver might be witness against them at the day of judgment if they deviated from the contract.... The circumstances of both are servile and mean. A. B. has deferred the consummation of the marriage, fearing he shall not be able to maintain her. He is unwilling to bring ruin upon her and his posterity and for that reason desires to stay single until fortune may favor them more.*

But P. S., a brisk young fellow settled in a pretty good way, has courted H. H. and desires to take her for better or for worse. She has naturally a greater fancy for the latter than the former and is afraid of losing such a good opportunity. Query: Should she wait for A. B.'s circumstances to improve? ... Or may she justifiably before God and man marry the latter, notwithstanding the solemn vows and imprecations made in the contract? She is under great perplexity of mind and soul.... She is resolved to be governed by your judgments, and to act as you prescribe.

A. If nothing more has passed between you and if A. B. is willing to release you fairly, without constraint, provocation, &c, we believe you may marry anyone else. But ... if A. B. will not give up his interest in you, you cannot honestly dispose of yourself otherwise, for your obligations were mutual.... Still, you'll do well to take the opinion of some able clergyman in the matter and not rely wholly on our answer. [Q.3, 17:10, 4 May 1695]

Q. *It was my fate to be courted by a young gentleman who so often vowed love and constancy that he prevailed with me not only to believe him, but to love him too. Knowing our love would disoblige our friends, we deferred our marriage. But we made mutual vows of constancy to one another as well as strict promises of marriage. . . .*

However, the spark soon after grew jealous of me and was confirmed in it by his rival, who boasted of favors he had never received from me. Nor would he believe me when I protested my innocence, although I gave him all the assurances of my fidelity and affection that virtue would permit. He decided to discharge me from my vow and never see me again, so I also discharged him and we parted. But soon afterward he began to court me again as passionately as ever. I desire your judgments whether we could void so solemn a vow and whether I may without perjury marry any other during his lifetime, since I have now plainly vowed never to marry him.

A. As we have often declared, you both were wrong to promise marriage against the consent of your friends, especially your parents. However, when it was done we think you could not undo it, we mean on both sides. After he had unjustly abandoned his vow, you could not be under any further obligation to him and were at liberty to marry any other. It's true you might have forgiven him and received him again had you seen any reason to do so, . . . but now you can't entertain him again without breach of your second vow. [Q.1, 17:14, 19 May 1695]

Q. *Some time ago I had frequent opportunities of conversing with a young gentlewoman of about 16, whom I liked extremely well. She had as much beauty, wit, and good humor as I could desire. That made me so pleased with her company that I endeavored to get more of it than in prudence I should have done. So her friends suspected I loved her and therefore took effectual means to deprive me of her conversation. . . . The separation awakened my affections and gave birth to a violent passion. For some time we have been corresponding, to my great satisfaction.*

I'm a younger brother and can maintain only myself like a gentleman, which I have honestly told her, and yet she seems to have no aversion for me. But she will have no inheritance until after a friend's death, and it may be some years before we can conveniently marry. I desire your advice whether we should in the meantime actually contract ourselves, or whether we should depend only upon each other's love and honor for our mutual security until that happy, happy time shall come, when we may with discretion marry?

A. Where there's honesty and sincerity, a contract is useless, for your mutual love is sufficiently obligatory. To honest persons such reciprocal favors bind as much as all the vows in the world. [Q.5, 18:17, 10 September 1695]

Q. *I have loved and am beloved by a gentlewoman of whose virtue I am very well satisfied. I have long courted her but without proposing marriage, for that would be very disadvantageous to me. Now I've met another woman of whose love I'm pretty well assured. The question is, should I shun the first (whom yet I love best) or no? If I marry her my friends will oppose the match, which I fear would ruin me. If I marry the second, they would be extremely pleased, for she has a considerable fortune and friends to help me. But then I must fear the ruin of the first, for she has a passionate esteem for me.*

A. It would be best if people would consider their circumstances before they give too much liberty to their passion, since in love as in war if they once engage it is very difficult to make an honorable retreat. Not making a formal proposition to the first lady does not matter, since courtship and keeping her company are sufficient to engage you too far to break off without her consent. If you can persuade her to release you (a request to which surely a sensible woman would agree, when a man desires it), it is best to marry to your greatest advantage. But if she refuses you, you're obliged in conscience to marry the first lady (or at least to remain single), whatever damage you may sustain by displeasing your friends. [Q.3, 18:22, 28 September 1695]

Q. *A young man under twenty happened to fall in love with a maid much older than himself, whom he courted for some time. He at last got her consent to make a pact with him to prevent each from marrying any other, and they wished that the party who married first might be debarred from heaven. The young man has since relinquished his pretensions to her, and his love is turned to such an extremity of aversion and hatred that he cannot now think of marrying her. He's twenty-five years old and is in love with another woman. He fully designs to make the other woman his wife unless your determination prevents him. I desire to know whether the wish is void, for it was made inconsiderately, rashly, in a heat, and underage. Marrying his first mistress, when he can't love her, would only make them both miserable. Wouldn't it be better to marry the second, whom he loves, so he may be happy with her, since he won't marry the former?*

A. If, as he says, he's already decided not to make her his wife whom he's obliged to marry and to marry another, ... why does he desire our opinion? But there's one phrase in the question—(unless our determination prevents him)—which it certainly will. The oath they both made is so solemn and the sanction so dreadful that we believe there's no room left for them to disentangle one another, even though they themselves were both willing. . . . And this binds more strongly on the man's side, because he was the one who prevailed with the woman to make such an oath. . . . As for it's being made underage, we wonder in what chapter in the Bible he finds it written that it's lawful to be perjured under one and twenty. . . . If the rashness, inconsiderateness, and heat with which a vow was made were enough to set a man clear of it . . . oaths and vows would be broken as soon as made and the very public faith of mankind vacated. . . .

However, we here readily grant . . . that had the first mistress played false, or run sheer away, . . . the man would be at his liberty to marry whoever he found to have him, for the obligation is certainly reciprocal.... This and such other instances should make people more cautious of such imprecations, lovers' vows being certainly registered in heaven, however they may be forgotten upon earth. Perjury in those cases is we believe the cause of many of those unfortunate marriages which are so frequently complained of. [*AO*, 2:96–98]

Q. *There was a maiden with whom I engaged so far in love that I promised her marriage and she the like to me, unknown to our friends. When they learned what we had done, they were very much troubled and have so far worked upon her that she has denied all that passed between us. She has told me positively she would never marry me. Now the question is: Am I at liberty to marry any other, she having freely discharged me in writing before witnesses?*

A. Without doubt she has made all your promises void.... Promises are always understood to be reciprocal.... Therefore, you are left to your discretion and if you have courage enough may venture the like repulse from another. [*AO*, 2:515]

Q. *A lady with her own and relations' consent not only admitted but gave all the encouragement to the address of a gentleman that a modest courtship would allow. After an examination of the estate and fortune and the approbation of both parties with their relations, the gentleman told the lady of his increasing love and begged an assurance from her ... that he might absolutely depend upon being happy with her as a wife. To that the lady kindly replied, "Sir, I'll promise you that if ever I marry any man breathing, it shall be yourself."... She since told several others that they were man and wife before God and she did fully resolve to have him.*

After this, the lady proving unkind, the gentleman took his leave.... The lady ... wholly cast off the gentleman, at the same time declaring ... that she only did it through the persuasion of a deaf half-Portuguese stepbrother, who has recently wheedled this

*lady to place her person and fortune into his own safekeeping.
As to her person, he has declared that he thinks it safest (for his
own advantage) for her to be kept single. Her fortune he has been
pleased to convert to his own use to make him a landed man
and a merchant.... He always seemed a public promoter of the
marriage until he found that his sister wanted to claim her money.
Then he privately forced her to break off vows and matrimony.
Gentlemen, your impartial answer is earnestly begged to the following questions:*

1. *Is this lady bound in honor and conscience to marry the
   gentleman?*
2. *If the lady should marry another man, are those promises
   made to the gentleman and attested by several witnesses a
   sufficient cause of divorce from the other man?*
3. *What the stepbrother (who is the originator of the unhappiness of both the gentleman and the lady in this affair) may
   justly deserve for his dishonest dealing?*

A. Your enemy is never the worse or more scandalous for being
either deaf or a half-*Portuguese*.... But to your questions:

To the first we answer: yes, if all is true as it is represented
and no material circumstance obliging the contrary has
been omitted. To the second, your own statement can supply you the affirmative,... provided the case be fairly stated,
but this depends upon the suspicion in the first answer.
To the last, we answer positively that you ought to treat
him with good language and persuade him if possible to
be just to her, which if he will not be and you have kindness enough for and interest with the lady, marry her and
then try, by the fair and proper means that your marriage
furnished you with, to make him honest whether he will or
no. [*AO*, 3:310–12]

Some correspondents explained that they had vowed never to
marry (or remarry) for various reasons and asked the Athenians'
opinions of the obligations or implications of such promises.

Questioners sometimes revealed that they did not regard personal vows of fidelity as the equivalent of formal weddings in church. The Athenians' answers thus had to address explicitly the relative status of private marital contracts and public ceremonies.

Q. *My fortune is not so great to place me in an eminent station…; my personage is indifferent. So I made a solemn vow never to marry, little thinking that it concerned anyone but myself. But (by what fate I know not) a young lady of a fortune far greater than mine expresses herself very much in love with me, insomuch that I have good reason to believe she will be either distracted or dead in a little time if I do not fulfill her desires.… The question therefore is: Will it be better to preserve the lady from what threatens her and break my oath or keep my oath inviolate and let the lady take her chance?*

A. We believe the vow being absolute to be obligatory upon you, since it's possible and was once in your own power. Nor can a probable misfortune like her death compensate for the guilt of your certain sin if you break it. But you can take other measures with the lady to abate her passion for you. You can visit only seldom and offer the greatest slights and affronts imaginable, provided you do not injure her reputation. We know someone who took this course in a like case, which proved effectual. [Q.4, 7:1, 29 March 1692]

Q. *Some years ago I became acquainted with a knot of good honest fellows, as merry, witty, and agreeable company (perhaps) as most in England.… They loved both their bottles and their mistresses; all were avowed bachelors and often painted marriage in the ugliest possible dress, with all the art of rhetoric imaginable. So I fancied marriage to be slavish, troublesome, and expensive, and the conversation of women dull and unedifying. I resolved against it, for I knew the pleasure of good company and the charms of wine, in addition to the easiness of a single life.… To hinder my weakness (as I then thought it) from ever entering into a state of life I thought so uneasy, I vowed against it, not considering the inconveniences of such a vow, nor that I should ever have as good an opinion of women as I now have.*

A. Our opinion is that his vow is not binding, for it was made upon false suppositions because marriage was misrepresented to him. Therefore, the motives and grounds of his vow being false ... it follows that the vow, having nothing to support it, falls with the error it was built upon. Had the querist had a true idea of marriage and been acquainted with his own inclinations, and had he made the vow on those grounds, it would certainly have been binding. [Q.9, 7:7, 19 April 1692]

Q. *Some time ago I buried my wife. When she lay upon her deathbed I vowed that if it pleased God to take her from me I would never marry again. But recently I lodged in a house where there is a young lady with a small fortune, whom I am very much smitten with. I have made my addresses to her and she has consented to live with me as a wife. We are taking one another's word; I have made a vow to be constant to her and she has made a vow to be true and faithful to me. I have likewise vowed, in case I die, to settle a yearly maintenance on her during her life and if she has any children by me, to settle them well in the world. I desire you to answer these two queries:*

  1. May I make that contract with this young lady and not break the vow I made to my former wife?

  2. And are the promises and vows we have made to each other as acceptable as marriage before God, in case we perform all things according to the uttermost of our powers?

A.1. You mistake the nature of your vow or you would recognize that this practice is as great a breach of it as you can possibly make. You undoubtedly planned it either to satisfy your wife that your children should not be wronged, if you have any; or if not, that no other woman should ever possess your esteem. The first possible motive was not altogether unreasonable, for second matches generally prove damaging to the first wife's children. But if your motive was the second, it was equally foolish for her to ask or you to offer such a promise, since no man knows one day what shall happen the next. You are obliged to marry if you cannot live honestly without a wife and might as well take one you like as any other.

A.2. No, they are not, since there remains undone that part which is necessary for decency and order. A marriage ceremony does not make you guilty of breaking your vow but gives a more lawful way to do so than by living in a continued act of fornication. Nor can any happiness be expected from a vicious contract. The gentlewoman has no reason to believe you will be true to her now that you have found a way to break your former promises. [Q.6, 12:11, 28 November 1693]

Q. *A gentlewoman had a very kind husband who died some years ago. She made a solemn vow that she would never marry again and to keep her vow she is now living with another gentleman she loves as man and wife but without marrying. Should she break her vow or continue to live as she does?*

A. Her vow is undoubtedly already broken. The only question is whether she should become honest. If she needs our assent to determine that, we shall not hesitate to affirm that she may safely marry, although it may be contrary to the fashionable opinion of the age. [Q.5, 15:6, 22 September 1694]

Other problems arose when one person changed his or her mind after making a solemn vow or contract for marriage and sought to—or perhaps actually did—marry another person. Much might depend on the exact nature of the promise, but the Athenians sometimes regarded even implicit promises as obligatory, at least to the extent of requiring a formal release.

Q. *A young man in love with a young gentlewoman promised her marriage without the knowledge of his own parents, although her parents did both know and approve it.... It happened that the young man being gone to travel found another occasion of marriage more pleasant to his fancy and more advantageous to his fortune. Now the question is: Whether without wounding his conscience and with the consent of his parents for the other, may he leave the former and take the latter?*

A. The prior obligation is still valid unless he can get a release from the former.... We think he is still obliged, although he did ill to promise without the consent of his own parents as well as hers. [Q.5, 5:13, 12 January 1692]

Q. *I promised a gentleman marriage. He went into Ireland and I received advice from a friend of mine that he was killed, whereupon I married another. Sometime later he came home.... I told him how it was and produced the letter. Now my husband is dead and he would have me to wife. Query: Am I obliged to have him?*

A. You may have him or another as stands best with your interest. [Q.7, 8:19, 1 November 1692]

Q. *A lady in her tender years by the many insinuations of a certain gentleman was inveigled to give a note under her hand that she would never marry any man but him. Now better information ... tells her that should she marry him she must forever render her life unhappy. And the gentleman refuses to release her promise, ... yet sometimes declares that he'll never have her or anything to do with her.... I desire to know whether his frequent declarations ... release her promise so that she may agree to the conjugal request of another.*

A. If you think you could live better with him than in a single state, offer him marriage before a witness. If he declines, you are free from him and may do what you please, for all such obligations are mutual.... There's no one can marry another against their will. We think this is the only method

to use other than choosing a single life, which you're at
liberty to do if you think it preferable. [Q.3, 9:11, 17 January
1693]

Q. *In the country I courted a maid of ordinary descent, who is no great
beauty and with a very slender fortune. I have said unto her that I
would like to make her my wife with the consent of my relations, ...
and she refused. . . . Now in the city I have a prospect of a woman
with a very good fortune, whom I can freely make my wife. . . . I
implore that you would answer if it is just in the sight of God to
marry the latter or no.*

A. We think in any cases of this nature all these promises, contracts, etc., either are actually mutual and equally binding or
are reasonably supposed to be so. Consequently, no person
is obliged any more than the other, for which cause we
think the querist is at liberty to embrace the second offer.
[Q.2, 10:13, 9 May 1693]

Q. *I'm the wife of a person of considerable estate and quality. Before I
married, I was courted by one much below me, and being overcome
by his importunity promised him marriage. But before the wedding
date was set, I was addressed by one with a fortune far beyond what
I could ever expect. And being ambitious of riches, I soon married
him, unknown to my former suitor, who on hearing thereof was
much surprised and accused me of horrid baseness. This is now
nearly ten years ago. . . . I'm so disturbed in my mind for what I've
done that I dare not receive the sacrament until I know how ... to
reconcile myself to God and my much-injured lover. Pray let me
have your advice as soon as possible, for I live in the country and
am now just going out of town.*

A. In the first place, you did very ill ... to forsake your first lover if
he gave you no provocation or just reason, especially on the
account of a fortune. . . . But marriage is like being born—
when once it's done, there's no undoing it unless death
loosens the hold. . . . You do ill in putting God and your

much-injured lover so near each other in your thoughts. Rather ask pardon ... for the wrong you do your much-injured husband thinking so much of any other. [Q.7, 10:14, 13 May 1693]

Q. *A friend of mine having a kindness for a young gentlewoman has entangled himself by keeping her company from time to time.... If he marries her he is undone, for she is no way suitable for him and all his friends are against it. He formerly promised her marriage, to which she made him no answer, but ... she now is willing.... May he lawfully refuse her, she not joining with him when he made her the promise, and having since told her that he could not marry her, his friends on whom he depends being against it?*

A. If he has engaged the young woman's affections and at the time he promised her marriage she gave him any equivalent assurance, even though not a formal promise, we think he can't handsomely or honestly leave her. Otherwise, we think he's at his own liberty. [Q.4, 11:17, 5 September 1693]

Q. *A friendship has been carried on between two persons of different sexes so far as that the fair party has yielded to the other's suit. She has by promise engaged herself to marry him within a convenient time and with parents' consent on both sides. After this, a breach was suddenly made on the woman's side without any reasonable cause given. Query: How far is a promise of marriage binding before God? Because it is generally said such persons are married in the sight of God. And if another person marries a woman that is so promised (knowing it beforehand) will he transgress the divine law? Your opinion is desired, for your judgment on the matter may either further or hinder an address to the above-mentioned fair party.*

A. It's true that the woman has an obligation not to marry any other but him to whom she promised, especially if with the parents' consent; nay, actually to marry him unless she has any valid reason against it. . . . But we think this obligation does not reach to another person. If he to whom she is promised will not relinquish his interest and release her from her promise, we should not advise any to make her his choice, because the justice of heaven may make her unhappy and then he must be also. [Q3, 11:24, 30 September 1693]

Q. *About four years ago I was courted by T. G., a sailor, to whom I engaged myself and he to me by breaking a piece of gold. Not long after, he went to sea. Then N. T. of the same profession courted me. I told him I was engaged, but at his desire I granted him the reversion of my favor after T. G.'s death. Then I was courted by I. S. (a seaman also). With him I broke a sixpence and positively engaged to marry him, having resolved to break my former engagements, which I did not tell him about.*

T. G. is dead and N. T. now claims my promise. . . . I do not intend to marry him . . . because I love I. S. much better. This is real truth and I need speedy advice about it. . . . Tell a troubled virgin what she should do. May I marry I. S. rather than N. T. . . . or perhaps should I marry neither?

A. Reversion of favors is such an uncertain sort of an inheritance that the hope of it could satisfy none but a madman or a stark lover, who are much the same. . . . Such an inconstant woman is likely to make any man unhappy. . . . You had no power to enter into any new obligations. . . . In the case of N. T., you made a promise of marriage after the death of T. G., and now that he is dead you are obliged to make it good. [Q3, 14:16, 14 July 1694]

Q. *I made a commitment to a woman in Flanders to wait some time for her in the hope she would consent to marry me, but we have no formal contract. In London, I have become acquainted with a young gentlewoman, whose obliging behavior has entirely won my affections. Her fortune, education, and personality in every respect meet my expectations. The only obstacle to a match is my commit-*

ment to the gentlewoman in Flanders. Can I with honor marry the Englishwoman before I return to Flanders? And if I have to return without doing so, should I clearly explain my present circumstances to the gentlewoman here, lest by expecting a commitment from me (which only my former promise would prevent) she slights other convenient matches now offered her by her friends, which may displease them and injure her own preferment?

A. If you don't go to Flanders, you should at least send word to the gentlewoman there and ask for her final decision, telling her truly the cause of your inquiry. Until you have done that, you cannot honorably proceed any farther with marriage here, for you have already made a little breach in honesty.... You should also speak plainly with the woman in town, and if she is worth loving, your sincerity will do you no injury. [Q.2, 15:1, 4 September 1694]

Q. *I am in league with a lady who unknown to me was previously engaged to another. She first showed kindness to me in such a remarkable way that it would have tempted any man.... The first gentleman learning of our relationship was much concerned and it's thought that he might die if he cannot have her. I am also so in love that I cannot part with her without risking the same hazard. I am resolved never to part with her unless it can be proved to be against the law of God. Now, gentlemen, I desire to know whether I may safely marry the lady with her consent, without committing a sin against God or a dishonorable act against the gentleman, for I did not know that they were engaged. Your speedy answer is desired, I being impatient till the doubt can be resolved.*

A. You can neither lawfully nor honestly have anything to do with her until her obligations to the gentleman are first canceled. If he agrees with us, that cancellation should not be very difficult to accomplish, since the love of an inconstant person is not worth preserving. You were in no way to blame for loving before you saw any reasons against it, but should you still pursue your passion with your mistress despite her former engagement, it would not only be ungenerous to the lover but also very displeasing to God Almighty. By their mutual vows and promises they have almost made it a marriage. [Q.4, 18:9, 13 August 1695]

Q. *It is the misfortune of a very fine and virtuous young lady to have contracted herself to a gentleman who now refuses to marry her or free her from her promise, but for what reason is unknown. He insults her and tells her she shall never marry while he lives, threatening that if she does he will sue her husband. I desire your advice how such a man may be obliged either to marry or free her, although I think she had better live in perpetual celibacy than make such a man her husband, for he already treats her in such a manner. Would a gentleman act contrary either to reason or religion if he should challenge him to fight? Your answer is earnestly desired.*

A. The spark who uses her so unhandsomely can have no excuse, and by his refusing to perform his part in the contract, he actually dissolves it. There's no question but the obligation is here mutual and reciprocal, tying one no more firmly than the other.... The lady had better never to have the comfort of matrimony at all than run such a desperate hazard to obtain it, we mean with one that has used her so ill already. Nor is there any need of her asking his leave to marry any other. As for his threatening to sue her husband, that's not like to frighten a man of sense and spirit, but rather the very opposition would make him more eager. As for fighting him and beating him into better manners, that might work in a camp but not in a country governed by steady laws, which if she can prove any damage we suppose will hardly deny her a remedy....

We have been more explicit in the present case because we must confess there is so great a temptation for a generous man (especially if there's any touch of love) to act too far in it. This much however he may do—discourse calmly with the gentleman, get his friends and those who have the most power over him to do the same, representing the unfairness and immorality as well as the unhandsomeness of his proceedings, and try if by that way they can bring him to release the fair lady out of his enchanted castle. If all this won't do, it's justice to publish his name, and let the world know what he is. (Send us the information, and we perhaps could help.) [*AO*, 2:73–74]

Q. *It was my fortune some time since to be in the company of a young lady who was with the liking and agreement of all friends just entering into the matrimonial state, so that it seemed to be a very happy match. . . . Some words of hers together with her pleasing company excited my lingering passion, and so puffed me up into a flame of love that I told her I wished the time might be come when both our hearts and hands should be joined, but I made no promise that I would do so. . . .*

The first time she saw her other spark she picked a quarrel with him and blasted all his hopes with a flat denial, swearing she'd keep his company no more, merely upon my account. Soon after, the time came when I had to leave on a long journey. At the first opportunity (about a fortnight later), I wrote to tell her that since my fate was uncertain she should not miss her opportunities upon my account, . . . intimating that I did not design to marry for some years yet. . . . Now this was some years ago and she still refuses all offers of marriage. I have a prospect of marrying where I may make a fortune, but the thought of her stops me and as it were damps all my proceedings. Therefore, I beg your advice whether I may with a safe conscience marry another, and what restitution I must make for my offense, and how I may ease myself from the thoughts of her who is far distant hence.

A. That you have injured the lady is very plain, since you have been in all probability the person that has not only hindered but perhaps ruined her fortunes, for her refusing to marry can only be upon your account. You have no way to free yourself but by finding her as good a husband as you have made her lose.... You can neither handsomely nor honestly leave unprovided for one who has left everything for you. [*AO*, 2:516]

Occasionally, property issues complicated marriage contracts.

Q. *A young lady had the misfortune of falling in love with a young gentleman, who contracted with her upon condition that if she was worth 500£, as she told him, he would marry her; if not, the contract was void. After they disagreed about something, the gentleman inquired after her fortune and learned she was worth little or nothing. Indeed, she confessed she was not worth much. Yet notwithstanding this the gentleman maintained her for six or seven years, but having had great losses was forced to go to Ireland. There he fell in love with a young lady worth 500£ and has her consent to be married. The query is whether this gentleman, since the contract with the other lady is void, may lawfully marry this young Irish lady? Pray your speedy answer for I am to give the gentleman notice by post of your opinion in the matter.*

A. As for the contract made only on condition of her being worth such a sum of money, it was of no force if the condition failed. But it's reasonable to inquire a little farther into what might be the obligations or reasons for his maintaining her so long. We think it was not the pure effect of gratitude for her love, but that rather it was for such favors received as did certainly give her a greater right to him than the utmost extent of the original contract could do. This he best knows, which alone ought to determine his actions. [Q.I, 17:17, 28 May 1695]

Q. *Before the day of marriage was set a London merchant, who was engaged to a virtuous lady with no great fortune, sustained such a great loss in the war that he could not pay off his full debts. But such was her affection for him that she promised to delay the wedding until he could settle his affairs with his creditors, which accordingly he has done.... But some of her friends have persuaded her that the settlement was extorted from his creditors and so he will not prosper in future. She is free to decide for herself but seems to want to disengage from her contract so that she could marry another man who has courted her in the meantime. Query: By the laws of God and all good men, is she obliged in honor and conscience to keep her contract with him if he does not resign his interest in her?*

A. If the lover tells his story right, we think instead of being free from him, his mistress is now more obligated to stand to the bargain. If she promised to have him while his affairs were dubious, she can have no pretense to leave him when they are settled. [Q.10, 18:12, 24 August 1695]

Q. *A young woman of passable beauty has an estate of over 1000£ inherited from some uncle or the like kin. At the importunity of her mother and other friends, she has engaged herself to her sister's husband's brother, who is agreeable to her neither in education, temper, or physiognomy, which contract or engagement now troubles her and causes her to doubt their mutual agreement.... She questions whether she should marry him, though some contracts have been made between them. But besides this a person that is much more equal to her believes he could obtain her consent.... What is best to be done in this case? That is, in conscience may the young man express his love and may she with safety leave the former based on her hesitations, even though all has been concluded but the ceremony?*

A. If this contract was made after she reached the age of discretion and she seemed to agree to it, it is still in force. But if it was extorted from her we believe she is not bound by it, although ... her conscience will be her witness.... If the first lover will set her at liberty, she can safely be free to do as she wishes. [Q.4, 18:17, 10 September 1695]

Q. *I courted a gentlewoman, but sometime later finding myself very much in debt, I acquainted her with my condition. She was in a way to live very well by her own industry and thinking me honest made me a promise to marry me whenever I had paid back the debt, even though I was not then worth a penny. But it being probable this will not be done soon, she begins to be weary of her promise. I desire your judgment whether she's obliged by it.*

A. Yes doubtless, because it was voluntary. Besides, it was made for such a good reason that it's a pity it should be broken. We think it important not to discourage this sort of honesty, of which we have too few examples. However, if there's no likelihood of your ever getting into such circumstances as she has made the condition of your marriage or not doing it for a long time, it would be generous of you to release her from her promise. But unless you do so, we think she cannot get free from its obligation. [*AO*, 2:156]

Correspondents sometimes wondered what could void a marriage contract, other than mutual consent. Sexual misbehavior by one party seemed an obvious answer.

Q. *Is fornication after a solemn contract as dissolving as adultery after marriage, and may the innocent party upon sufficient proof and detection of the fornication be at liberty to contract again with another or marry if they think it fitting?*

A. We see no reason at all that after such a violation of the contract it should remain obligatory; for by such an action the person offending is made one flesh with a third person and therefore the obligation to that is yet stricter than a bare promise to the first. . . . As to the latter part of the question, whether the innocent person may be at liberty to contract again—we answer, yes . . . the liberty is much greater here than the law will give in the case of marriage. . . . Here the law has nothing at all to do, and persons may act according to their conscience and the law of God. [Q.3, 3:24; undated, after 26 September 1691]

Q. *A man contracted to a virtuous gentlewoman was troubled about some unjust actions he had formerly committed. He revealed his discontent to her but promised to make a full restitution to all that he had wronged and immediately did so. However, it's so great a trouble to her to find herself engaged to a man guilty of such crimes that she thinks she may justly free herself from all the promises to be his wife. The question is if a man who has made a voluntary restitution without any compulsion but that of his conscience and firmly resolves never to commit the least injustice again ought to be treated as a dishonest person, . . . and if this is a just cause for her to disengage herself from him? A speedy answer is desired, for the parties concerned refer themselves to your determination.*

A. Where should a lover trust a secret if not where he loves? It's but a very poor return to reject him for the highest voluntary evidence of his confidence and esteem. . . . He's good and virtuous and this should chain her to him more closely than before. Repentance is a lovely virtue, and it ought not to be frowned upon but to be encouraged and rewarded and given a new title to her heart. [Q.4, 6:7, 23 February 1692]

Q. *I was sometime since contracted to a lady of beauty, wit, and reputed virtue, but a little before the time appointed for marriage, I myself found her in bed with a young fellow. I have no room to doubt her dishonesty. The query is, am I now bound to perform my contract?*

A. No certainly, . . . since had you been actually married, this crime would have dissolved the contract even more surely than was the case before consummation. [Q.6, 6:17, 22 March 1692]

Q. *I unfortunately contracted myself to a young lady whom I always believed virtuous, but I am since credibly informed of the contrary.*

I desire your advice if I'm obliged to perform the contract ... and if not, in what manner may I handsomely get free?

A. Be as sure as you can that the report is not a scandal and the lady wronged by it, for some malicious person might want to hinder your marrying her. If you are satisfied the story is true, you may send her this *Mercury* as a final adieu. [Q.6, 14:6, 9 June 1694]

CHAPTER 5

"Both Sides Must Make Allowances"

MATRIMONY

WHEN THE ATHENIANS ADDRESSED the issue of marriage itself, they sometimes had to begin at the very beginning: What constituted matrimony? In a country lacking a comprehensive legal definition, it was hardly surprising that people became confused and occasionally referred to multiple possible spouses. Letters and responses alike referred to marriages according to "the law of God," "the law of nature," or "the law of the land." The Athenians answered such questions inconsistently. Commonly, they stressed the need for complete, voluntary religious marital rituals, but they also on occasion regarded explicit or implicit contracts and the initiation of sexual relationships as definitive.

Correspondents who inquired about behavior within matrimony had wide-ranging questions. Some lamented having selected the wrong spouse (including a wife already pregnant by another man) and asked for advice about dealing with the consequences. Many described contentions over the control of marital property; others complained of abusive behavior or infidelity, suggesting the possibility of separation or divorce. And a few asked whether married couples could attempt to avoid the births of children they could not afford to raise.

Q. *Are marriages of underage persons lawful? This question is based on an observation of the ill success of such marriages.*

A.   One and twenty is the age appointed by the laws of our nation . . . though the law of nature has perhaps fixed a far shorter limit. A marriage before the laws of the land would permit . . . may be reckoned valid, though not legal in respect of that law. Yet at the same time it may be both valid and legal, too, if we consult the law of nature, which prevents none from marrying who are old enough for the ends thereof. [Q.10, 1:13, 5 May 1691]

Q.   *A young man being gone to sea and staying there from his wife eighteen months, she in the meantime marries another. Query: At the return of the first husband, whose wife shall she be?*

A.   If the first were really and effectually married to her, she must be his still, if he has a mind to take her again and thinks her never the worse for wearing. [Q.13, 3:4, 8 August 1691]

Q.   *A woman married a husband who soon after went upon a trading voyage for Virginia, intending to return back in a year's time, but has been absent from her for above these eight years. Neither has she received any letter from him in all the time. And not knowing whether he be dead or alive, . . . she desires to be informed whether she may lawfully marry another man?*

A.   The law provided formerly seven years, after which it supposed the man dead. . . . If she means by lawfully, according to our law, she may marry another. But we can't promise her free by the law of God, which nowhere makes such an exception. . . . We can say no more but desire her to secure the quiet of her conscience and advice from the ecclesiastic authority, since the law gives her the liberty she wants. [Q.3, 4:7, 20 October 1691]

Q.   *I had the fortune to be joined in matrimony to a man who had another wife and children by her, which I discovered and brought an indictment against him. . . . After he was convicted of bigamy I begged he might be transported to the colonies rather than hanged, which was granted. Sometime after, I had an account of his death and was married some years after his supposed death to another. I lived comfortably with that husband for more than two years when I received a letter from my first husband courting me for my company, asking that I go overseas and live with him, etc. Query: Which of the two (if both alive) is my real husband? Which of them ought I to follow, or ought I to shun both?*

A. The first was not your husband before God, he being another woman's at the same time, for God can't be the author of adultery. Nor could he be your husband in the eye of the law, being legally dead because of the death sentence before his transportation. [Q.1, 4:24, undated, after 28 November 1691]

Q. *About three years ago I was privately married to a young man without my friends' consent or knowledge. He promised he would not bed with me until he had performed a journey which he was to take, neither did he. He soon went on his journey and did not return until about a year ago. During his absence I was importuned and married to another man and had a child with him before the other came back. We are all three in trouble of mind about it. Now I desire to be satisfied about it by you. . . . Which of these men is my real husband, seeing the first never bedded with me?*

A. By the law of God the first is your husband; by the law of the land, the last. By the same law that you belong to the first, he may disengage himself from you or may retain you, but by the law of the land he can't do the last. The best method we know is that you beg pardon both of God and him. As for his case, we believe he has no reason to trouble himself about it, since he is not only at liberty to marry whom and when he pleases, but to thank God that he has escaped such a partner; for . . . so much folly or impiety was no promising omen. [Q.10, 9:12, 21 January 1693]

The Athenians usually affirmed that a proper religious ceremony was required for a valid marriage, but that sexual relations were not necessary.

Q. *A gentlewoman forced by her guardian to marry one she never liked steals out after dinner and marries her longtime servant, who beds her immediately. Query: Whose wife is she? Can the first husband oblige her to live with him she does not love?*

A. Many an unhappy marriage is thus made and young persons ruined by the treachery and covetousness of guardians.... But in the present case the lady took an effectual course, though we think the day before would have been much better than an hour after.... If she were really forced by her guardian to do what she did ... then the former marriage, or rather ceremony, is null and void, as we think the force makes it. And the second must necessarily remain good, and the lady must be his wife. [Q.4, 6:17, 22 March 1692]

Q. *A person was some time ago married to a young woman, but not bedded. She did after marriage solemnly promise that she'd never alter what she had done, but at a certain time would come and live with him. The time appointed is now come, but her mind is so changed that she declares she'll never come near him. Query: Can she do this lawfully?*

A. No, doubtless, neither by the laws of God nor of man; the strong words passed between them and they made a contract both civil and sacred. [Q.2, 15:20, 10 November 1694]

As the Athenians also declared in the context of considering pledges by those who had vowed not to remarry, private vows were inadequate without a formal public ceremony.

Q. *A gentleman to obtain his desires of a young lady, after several promises of marriage, takes a Bible and reads the marriage vows, declaring themselves man and wife in the presence of God Almighty....*

He passed for her husband, living with her several years and had two children by her. But ... they fell out and parted, and the gentleman is married to another. The question is, which of the two is his lawful wife before God?

A.   If people after all will take no warning, but still go on thus to cheat the parson, they must even thank themselves, and take what follows. [Q.6, 10:7, 18 April 1693]

Q.   *If a woman and I have promised to live together faithfully like man and wife, according to the laws of matrimony, is the carnal knowledge of one another in that case fornication?*

A.   We have often enough answered to cases of this nature and again reply that if it be not fornication, it is a great folly in both of you, for she may leave you or you her, which is most likely. Such instances are frequent.... The injury may be to your children if you have any.... It's a sin, because against the just laws of the nation you live in, ... and it's against the custom of all civilized nations ... who have made matrimony a solemn and public thing, to prevent innumerable inconveniences. [Q.4, 11:1, 11 July 1693]

Q.   *A man courted a young woman for a considerable time. He made a great many protestations of eternal faith and sincerity, and then one Sunday night he and two of his brothers forcibly carried her to a church. There the reader recited part of the matrimonial service, but they had no ring. After that they returned her as they found her, everyone going to his own house. A year later, his father's servant bore him a child. After that the young woman came to London and has not seen him in seven years.... She desires to know if she may safely marry another?*

A.   It seems in this pretended marriage there was neither her consent, a ring, nor any further consummation, all of which were necessary to make it valid. Therefore, she may marry in earnest as soon as she can get anyone to agree. [Q.6, 16:13, 29 January 1695]

Q. *I must beg your opinion concerning an unhappy gentlewoman*
    of my acquaintance, who had a child by a man who then left her
    miserable. Another gentleman fell in love with her but would not
    marry her because he knew her former misbehavior. Still, they
    made strict vows to God and each other in a church and at several
    other times, after which he owned her for his wife to all the world.
    They have had several children. Neither broke their vows but they
    live faithfully with each other. They have not gone through a formal
    marriage ceremony because he can't bear the reproach it would be
    to him as a very high-spirited and passionate man. She is certain
    of his fidelity, but she wants your advice about her religious status.
    May she take holy communion? The ceremony of the matrimonial
    words is only law. The vow to God is everything and they have not
    broken it.

A. You seem to argue very warmly for your acquaintance, as if
    you were nearly concerned in the matter. But that does not
    make a difference. . . . Nothing is more common than the
    case you describe. It's impossible to tell how many thou-
    sands have been ruined by the same methods. . . . Nothing
    can be clearer than that she lives in fornication. Some so-
    lemnity before witnesses has been in all nations accounted
    necessary for matrimony. . . . Our country requires a public
    contract for life as essential to marriage. . . . Whoever is in
    adultery or any other grievous sin must repent before they
    come to communion, unless they'd eat and drink their own
    damnation. She shows no repentance while she persists in
    her sins. [Q.1, 16:26, 16 March 1695]

Yet circumstances could lead to a different verdict on the validity of a marriage begun with sexual relations and not including
a public ceremony. The next example is a unique three-letter
sequence. Some spelling errors in the first letter have been re-
tained despite editing because of the Athenians' comments on
them in the first response.

Q. *I have been in love this three years, almost to distraction—I have had one child by him I love so dear. He is very civil to me but visits me very seldom unless I send to him, and then he is angry, then am I on ten thousand racks, and could murder myself. I have been advised by all my friends never to see him more. I have strived to do it, but can't, for if he's from me but a week, I think it an age. . . . Now gentillmen, I beg your answer what I must do in this cease, leave him I never can. All I desire is that he will never marry unless it is to me, or else never forsake me, for if he do, I shall sartainly murder myself. I bags your advise in your next* Mercury—*thus bagging your pardons, I hope you will give a charitable anser to a discontented womans question.*

A. If the querist had not specified her character and quality, it might have been guessed at without much difficulty by her way of spelling and writing. She's infected with the two greatest plagues of her sex, prostitution and love. . . . Why should the poor cheated creature expect that a man should continue to be true when he has more than all he desires? Oh how can she wonder that any is false to her when she has already been so to virtue? . . . Nor is it any wonder that she should have no other thoughts but those black and horrid ones of despair and murder. . . . Her desire that he should still live as he does with her argues impenitence for her crime, and that she still desires to continue in it. . . .

It's then a clear case that there remains but one way for her to save her soul, . . . and that is immediately to leave him, unless he'll immediately marry her, not trusting his promises or continuing one moment longer in so damnable a sin. . . . This question we have thus at large discoursed on, because the disease is so epidemic. [Q.1, 9:3, 20 December 1692]

The second version, obviously edited and revised by the Athenians (and sharply edited here), was published exactly a week after the first without admitting the repetition. Negative reaction from readers (or possibly one of the Athenians themselves) on the censorious initial response can be inferred. This time they offered the woman some advice on dealing with her lover, not just condemnation for her misbehavior.

Q. *I have been in love this 3 years, and in this time I have had one child by him I loved, and now I find he begins to slight me. . . . I am the most miserable of all my sex. . . . Should he persist in his unkindness, it will certainly make me commit violence on myself. . . . I am desperate and do not care what becomes of me . . . Therefore, as you are Christians, send your speedy answer, which may be a means to save the soul of a desperate, discontented woman.*

A. It's a lack of the true sense of religion and fear of God that has brought these excessive troubles upon you. . . . Our advice is immediately to beg pardon of God for your follies and impieties and live more strictly and religiously than you have done. . . . Your business is to slight him as the author of your shame and disquiet. . . . Never admit him either to a common friendship or much more to his ancient familiarities unless he forthwith marries you. If he really esteems you, he'll not refuse it. . . . Perhaps there can be nothing more serviceable to you than often to reflect upon his ingratitude and baseness, qualifications that render him unfit for a relationship with any reasonable person. [Q.4, 9:5, 27 December 1692]

When the man joined the dialogue more than two weeks later, the Athenians learned that parental disapproval of a potential marriage had played a major role in creating the young people's anguish. They proclaimed the woman and her lover to be married in every way that mattered and expressed sympathy for her. In this instance the Athenians decided that mutual consent and the onset of sexual relations trumped the need for a religious ceremony, although in other responses they said the opposite.

Q. *I am the unfortunate man. . . . I acknowledge myself guilty and heartily repent of my fornication, resolving never to do the like again, but how to disengage myself from her I know not. I love her and have promised to marry her, against which my aged parents are so averse, that they threaten me with their deepest curses if ever I marry her. Nay (which is worse), my father says it will bring his gray hairs to the grave. Sirs, I humbly beg your advice in this case and will follow your directions and forever remain your obliged humble servant.*

A. Our judgment upon it is that the whole affair ought not to have been carried on, but . . . it's a marriage already, as to the essence, ends, and design of marriage. It is only sinful by accident, as being against the just laws of the nation, which require public solemnization. . . . The paternal power is very sacred. However, . . . it's impossible for the young man to obey his father in not marrying, since it's done already. The public ceremony . . . is only a solemn attestation of marriage, but not marriage itself. . . . Next, the parents' injunction in this case is also sinful in offering such injustice to the woman, for what other satisfaction can be made her? So that our advice is that either the man cohabit with her secretly, if the parents are irreconcilable . . . or if they may be brought to consent, let them marry forthwith publicly. . . . We desire to hear what is done further in the matter. [Q.2, 9:10, 14 January 1693]

The Athenians offered more consistent answers to general questions about matrimony.

Q. *Do most persons marry too young?*

A. There being so many unhappy marriages . . . we may conclude most persons marry too young. . . . Though on the whole, I don't look upon marrying too young to be the vice of this age, when it's so hard a matter to persuade people to marry at all. [Q.5, 1:13, 5 May 1691]

Q. *Is the woman's condition in marriage worse than the man's?*

A. That's much as she manages it. Nature has generally given the fair sex art enough ... by which if either she herself or custom or law has given ours any advantage, they may if they please recover more than their own again. In childbirth only they have much the heavier part of the load. [Q.6, 1:13, 5 May 1691]

Q. *What's to be thought of a wife who forsakes her husband for his poverty?*

A. Hardly anything bad enough, if that poverty was not his fault or continued by his own carelessness or wickedness. [Q.15, 1:21, undated, after 23 May 1691]

Q. *Should a man neglect his children by a first wife to please a second, when nothing else will do it?*

A. That wife is not worth pleasing who requires such wicked, unreasonable terms. [Q.1, 1:23, undated, after 23 May 1691]

Q. *Why does love generally turn to coldness and neglect after marriage?*

A. Had the question been proposed universally, we must have denied it. . . . But the question is very cautiously and prudently put. . . . One great cause we believe to be the custom of the age. We have seen some kings' reigns wherein it has been thought an abominable scandal for a man to love his own wife. . . . And a larger cause than this we have now identified. Variety has a strange charm in it. . . . Satiety commonly breeds loathing and even manna every day would make one weary of it. But this variety may be obtained, this satiety may be cured, where there is at first a virtuous love grounded on sympathy and similitude as well as wit and discretion. . . . Discretion hides those faults that are generally revealed after marriage or removes them by degrees, and wit has always something entertaining and new.

That's the spirit which keeps the sweets of matrimony from growing vapid, dull, and disagreeable. [Q.3, 2:13, 7 July 1691]

Q. *Would the Athenians… make singular good husbands, for they have such a great measure of Christian patience toward their querists?*
A. The thanks of the house to you… the surest way to resolve the query is to ask their wives. [Q.4, 11:19, 12 September 1693]

Q. *Is it just that a poor, innocent cuckold should bear the infamy when the persons who confer that title upon him seem to be the only guilty parties?… And how many different circumstances might be involved?*
A. Some are in this number and are ignorant of it. Some think they are, but are not; those men are more miserable than if they really were and didn't know it…. Others are cuckolds but will not believe it because of the good opinion they have of their wives. Some know it and do all they can to hinder it, but others both know and would prevent it if it were in their power, which indeed are the most unhappy of all…. The husband deserves no infamy in the matter unless his own perfidy or ill treatment of his wife has partly caused her to accept the addresses of another…. Although the wife in such cases is not excusable, the husband may justly be blamed, because he brought it upon himself. When the man performs his part of the marriage covenant, he is undoubtedly free from any disgrace from the ill conduct of his wife. [Q.4, 17:11, 7 May 1695]

Q. *You are desired to give a reason why most men before matrimony try to be agreeable and good-humored especially during courtship, but when once they have achieved their aim of marriage they grow morose and careless, and that which seemed the only object of their wishes becomes often their greatest aversion or at least indifference.*

A. Suppose another querist should ask the same about the ladies, why are they less careful to please after marriage than before? Then the same answer might serve for both. They have caught the fish and the net may be thrown under the table. But there are other reasons. Difficulty whets, sweetens, and endears; satiety cloys. Before marriage all put their best side forward but afterward persons are more intimately acquainted. ... A thousand little cross accidents sour both parties. Both sides must make allowances for faults if they want to live happy. Possibly they expected more from each other than is to be found below the moon and therefore are angry when they find themselves disappointed and mistaken. [Q.4, 17:27, 2 July 1695]

Q. *Can a man divorce his wife in case of fornication and not break the commandments of God?*

A. No doubt the querist takes fornication here in the largest sense. ... We think there's no question but that according to the laws of nature, the law of God, and the Christian law, as well as the laws of our own and almost all other lands, he may be divorced for that reason, or rather the marriage is actually dissolved by such a breach of the conjugal vow. But here the man is not permitted to be judge himself, for then perhaps we should have divorces every week, as often as men grow weary of their wives. ... An action of this sort ought to have legal proof and to be performed in a legal way, since it's not fair that the person should be plaintiff, judge, and executioner. [*AO*, 1:62]

People who believed they had made the wrong choice of a spouse expressed their regret and asked the Athenians for advice.

Q. *Three years past, having an old father that intended to exceed the years of Methuselah, I out of despair (because he did not allow me a handsome maintenance) married an old, decrepit superan-*

nuated maid with a very good fortune, who was very sickly. Since then she has so perfectly recovered that I have reason to fear she'll even imitate my father. . . . Advice to an almost distracted man. . . . First, is it a crime to borrow some of my father's buried gold? . . . Second, my old wife so drafted agreements by my own consent before marriage that I resigned all over to her disposal. . . . Now, because I know where to seize them may I not commit them to the flames and take possession of all?

A. Two hard cases. . . . In our judgments it is a clear case your father's . . . property is still his and he is your father. . . . For your spouse, we think the case is harder. If she allows you sufficient funds to live like a gentleman, you have no reason in the world to complain. . . . If she refuses to let you have what's truly necessary and convenient for you (not for your extravagancies), we think (though we may be mistaken) that it is lawful for you to burn the agreements. Our reason is that a husband seems to have a right to the goods of the wife. . . . It seems preposterous and unnatural in such a case that an inferior relation should have power to preclude a superior from a proportion of what should be in common between them. [Q.1, 10:1, 28 March 1693]

Q. *I am a widow of no fixed place of abode. I have been beloved by an ingenious man for some years; he now is married to a good, discreet woman. But she is old. He can't love her but still really dotes on me so much so that he is almost lunatic and disturbed in his mind. I am afraid my unkindness to him in not marrying him while we were both single will break his heart. . . . I am satisfied he really loves me. . . . If I had had him, because our age, quality, and fortune agreed, we might have been happy enjoying each other, but now he is ruined by my ingratitude. When he was most loving, I was most unhappy and in a bad mood. I am heartily sorry for making him unhappy and causing his misfortunes. Therefore, let me beg your speedy directions what I should do to make him satisfaction for the injury I have done to him.*

A. You must do all that lies in your power to render him happy, for which there is but one way and that is by doing his duty. You ought indeed to beg his pardon.... Urge his obligations of love and tenderness to his wife, whose age ought to have been considered before marriage and can be no excuse to him now. Prevail on him to divert and conquer all the irregularity of his love for you. The best way to achieve that end is by moving so far away from him that he may neither ever hear from you or know where you are. You should tell him this lest his passion should be continued by his having any hopes of seeing you again. [Q.7, 18:14, 31 August 1695]

Sometimes questioners expressed concern about legal issues involving marriage, either under English or biblical law. One involved the prohibition in the Old Testament against marrying sisters, even if the first one died.

Q. *Should mutual consent dissolve the marriage contract, since... that could unmake all other contracts? And were it not better for public society if it were so?*

A. It was not man that made the law of marriage but God, who said it was not good for man to be alone. And as he had power to make such a law, he had power to repeal it, which he has done under such conditions as adultery, etc.... This is not like other contracts, as the querist urges, since God... has taken this into his own particular care. [Q.6, 4:2, 3 October 1691]

Q. *I have married a man of contrary opinion in religion to my own. Query: May I lawfully bring up the children in my own opinion unknown to him, though he be utterly against it?*

A. The resolution of this query depends upon facts. If you are of the right religion, you ought undoubtedly to bring up the children in the same, if possibly you can.... The nearest to it is the present doctrine and established discipline of the

Church of England (if we did not think so, it would be a shame for us to be members of it). [The last sentence comes from a later answer in the same issue.] [Q.1, 10:2, 1 April 1693]

Q. *A gentleman has married two sisters in succession. He had one child by the first, but it was stillborn. After her death he married the second and has had six children by her. They have lived apart for some years. Now they desire your advice whether they may lawfully come together again or marry any other persons. There was a kind of a contract between him and the second before he married the former.*

A. If any real contract passed between him and the second, he is the worse for breaking it and marrying the first. However, when that was actually done and consummated, he forever prevented himself from marrying the second without a breach of both his country's laws and the laws of God.... The scripture is plain.... From what has been said, it follows that they cannot lawfully come together again, but are at liberty ... to marry others. [Q.1, 18:13, 27 August 1695]

Q. *Is it permissible to court a married woman with a plan to marry her after her husband's death? And is a contract made with her obligatory?*

A. It's so far from being permissible to court a married woman that it is a crime to love or desire her, for it is a plain breach of the Tenth Commandment, if not of the Seventh, nay, the Sixth, too, since it's hardly possible to love the wife without wishing for the husband's death.... But if in spite of virtue and common prudence they have made a promise or contract for when the woman's at liberty, we do think such a contract or promise obligatory though impermissibly made. [Q.2, 18:22, 28 September 1695]

Three men complained that they had married women who were already pregnant by others, with many ensuing complications.

Two servants claimed they had been deceived by masters who had impregnated their brides.

Q. *I am a person of a very fair estate.... I married a young woman who had nothing but her beauty and seeming virtue to recommend her, though of birth and quality equal to mine.... I had not the least whispering jealousy of her lewdness or dishonesty, but I was quickly undeceived and found by tokens evident enough that she was no maid.... Five months had scarce run out before my virtuous spouse was brought to bed, dying herself the very moment of her delivery, and leaving me the unhappy keeper, not the father, of a son....* Queries:*
   1. *Should this child inherit my estate or any part of it?*
   2. *Am I obliged to take any more care of him than of a stranger laid at my door?*
   3. *May I justly dispose of him to those wandering people, who for a small piece of money take children and educate them as their own, and so to rid myself forever of that which would otherwise be a perpetual shame and trouble to me?*

A. To the first query: Neither...supposing the case really be as you present it.... But if the lady brought any fortune, we think the case is something altered, for he is certainly her child though not yours.

   To the second... He is more to you, for he was born in your house and would ... in law recover the estate if born in wedlock....

   Third, No, for the innocent child will have a very hard fortune to be bred a rogue because his mother was a _____.... But there is a middle way.... You may convey him immediately to some honest though poor person at a distance from yourself, and there let him have honest education without knowing what he is, until of age to go abroad. Then you may put him young to some master of a ship and oblige him to leave the boy in the West Indies or some remote place, having taken care there for his subsistence, giving him something therewith to begin in the world. [Q.6, 10:30, 8 July 1693]

Q. *I came in a very mean condition to a small garrison in their majesties' dominions, where I became a servant to the lieutenant, who was a housekeeper and a person of good influence and power in that place. After some time continuing in this service (by my master's encouragement and content), I married my fellow servant. The ceremony was performed by a minister very indecently, not in the church but in a mean room in my master's house. Being thus married, I found my wife with child by my master, which for his honor and my own reputation I concealed and owned the child. I lived with the woman at least 7 or 8 years, in which time I had 3 children by her, who I know are my own.... My master, in order to make me amends ... for taking such cracked ware off of his hands, helped me into some posts of good advantage to me, whereby I was enabled to live handsomely and saved money.*

But my master dying about 2 years ago, I fell deeply in love with a man's daughter of the place.... She loves me (I believe) with much ardency and sincerity; with this woman I have laid myself under the sacred obligation of a solemn oath to be true and constant to her, as she has likewise reciprocally done to me. Though I have relinquished my former wife, I resolve (if my ability continues) to maintain her and her children and accordingly do so. Now since I am censured for my actions by some people, I desire your answer to these following questions....

According to the law of conscience, matters of divorce being so tedious and chargeable ... may I live with this woman (as my real wife in the sight of God), with whom I keep company? If in your judgment I live in a sinful state with this woman, will God charge my oath against me if I should endeavor to break off with her? If it be a sin, I beg you to deal honestly by me in laying before me plainly and effectually the consequences of it. Gentlemen, I have been as just on all sides in stating my case, as possibly I could with brevity. I desire your speedy answer.

A. (Q.1) No, by no means, as you will answer it at the day of judgment. Since you pretend to deal plainly with us and to want our advice, remember... that it will be adultery in you. God will judge whoremongers and adulterers. Do not deceive yourself. You cannot proceed in such conduct and be saved....

(Q.2) Will any brutal enjoyments or blinded passions... countervail the loss of your reputation, the wounds of your conscience, the injury you do your lawful wife, and the unhappy expectation of just retributions hereafter? Certainly, you have abandoned your pretensions to reason and religion....

(Q.3) We have dealt by you as you have desired and do further declare that whatever vows you have made to this second woman are void.... We advise you to go home, beg your wife's pardon, admonish the other woman of her sin, and by a better life show the evidence of your repentance toward God and the world, which you have injured by your example. [AO, 2:5-7]

Q. *It was the misfortune of a friend of mine to marry a woman who was two months gone with child by her master. That ruined my dear friend, for he parted from her as soon as he conveniently could after he found it out. Because she dealt with him so treacherously, he could not love her, nor still cannot. It was almost two years ago that they parted, neither does he own her for a wife, but desires to be free from her. Even so she has a good friend in her master, who gives her money and has admitted fathering the child.... He has also given the best part of 100£ toward bringing up the child. Yet they threaten my unfortunate friend with gaol, running him into debt and all the misery imaginable because he left her. He keeps the matter private, but is very uneasy in this dangerous condition and knows not how to come out of it, unless your advice can direct him. Q: Whether according to the law of God he is free in conscience to give her a bill of divorce.*

A. Our Savior, who was the best expositor of the law, has forbid divorcement upon any account whatever except in the case of adultery. In such an accident as this, there's no remedy but silence and patience, for maintain her he must, she being lawfully his wife. . . . She is not accountable to him for what was done before marriage. If she has been an honest woman since, he has nothing against her. But if he can prove the contrary by good witness, he may have relief in an ecclesiastical court. If not, there is nothing else to be done but to take her and endeavor to live quietly together. [*AO*, 2:63]

Correspondents requested advice about behavior within marriage. Often, disputes arose between husbands and wives over property, with the Athenians usually supporting the husband. But in the first example below, the Athenians warned a woman about retaining documents related to a former lover, who might then retaliate against her by damaging her reputation.

Q. *Should a young lady in reason or prudence retain any letters or pictures of any former lovers after she's married?*
A. It may seem in itself an indifferent thing unless some circumstances totally alter the case. One is if the husband is inclined to jealousy. Another is if the lady when married loved any other person more than her husband. . . . There may yet be one case more . . . and that is, when there's a probability such persons may think or speak unhandsomely of her if she keeps such things. Being enraged by her action . . . they might easily enough do just that. [Q.14, 3:4, 8 August 1691]

Q. *A gentlewoman marries; the husband by contract is to leave her so much at his death if she survives him. She plans to deposit a parcel of her husband's goods in a friend's hands to be there kept for her own use without the husband's knowledge. This I fear is a thing too much practiced by wives in this great city and elsewhere, to the great damage (and sometimes ruin) of their husbands. Therefore, your resolution is desired: Is this unlawful for both the wife and the receiver? This question and your solution I am sure may be of great use to the public.*

A. Theft on either side is very base and unjust, since what is the husband's is the wife's. . . . But the injustice is worse on the woman's side, since the law can only touch the husband, who is answerable both for his own and his wife's actions. . . . In justice neither man nor wife has power to dispose of a farthing without each other's concurrence. . . . We don't deny but in some cases such secret securing of one party's separate interest without giving the other any account may be very just, virtuous, and prudent. . . . For instance, when either the man or the wife run into debt willfully . . . ruining themselves and their families. [Q.2, 5:9, 29 December 1691]

Q. *Is it a breach of the marriage vow for a man to keep his money from his wife so that she does not have the full command of it as well as he?*

A. No: Because she does not understand his employment or how to dispose of it as well as he can. He can be jailed for debts, and therefore he must have the full disposal of their income. [Q.6, 8:24, 19 November 1692]

Q. *If a man has an only daughter and marries her to a shopkeeper whose business goes bankrupt but lives well on his estate, may he detain this daughter lawfully from her husband? And if he may, is there any way for a man to recover his wife again?*

A. Nothing ought to separate those whom God has joined, unless it be a cause indeed of very great weight and moment. We here suppose extreme lewdness, absolute carelessness to maintain a wife and children, or such intolerable abuses as put her really in danger of her life. We question whether any other causes can be sufficient when a marriage is valid.

For the way of recovering such a wife again, you may consult our former volumes. [Q.2, 10:5, 11 April 1693]

Q. *When I went to Flanders in my post as an army captain under the king and queen, I was in love with a woman. My absence so increased my affection for her that I left my command to return to England to marry her. Since our marriage my wife has become so fond of my presence that (notwithstanding a new commission I obtained through influence) she will not agree that I should hazard myself in the army. To avoid my going again during the last campaign, she persuaded me to pay for leave to stay at home.... Now this has led to some criticisms of me, specifically that I have misbehaved by taking the king's money yet have refused to venture my person for the good of my country with the rest of my fellow soldiers. I therefore desire for the satisfaction of my wife (who will not be prevailed upon by any argument of mine) to give your opinion whether I ought to be governed by her any longer in a matter that so nearly concerned my honor.*

A. You can neither honorably nor honestly receive the king's pay without fulfilling your duties, which include fighting if the situation arises. Nor can you leave your wife without her consent, for you are no longer wholly at your own disposal. We think it would be reasonable for her to support your going,... and it's probable that absence would again rekindle that love which wedlock and time too often bring to an end.... But if neither these or any other arguments can prevail with your wife, you must make the best of what you have. Then by all means leave your post so you can be replaced by one who may be more capable of performing it. [Q.2, 14:2, 26 May 1694]

Q. *I recently married a widow who was a sole trader in the city for many years, making good profits ... but soon after our wedding when I refused to grant her an unreasonable request, she quit her trade, carried away her goods to places to me unknown, and altered her debt-book.... She from time to time has also secretly carried away my plate and goods. And has twice since left me for a month at a time ... she's now gone for a third time. Pray, gentlemen, advise me in this affair: How may I preserve myself from the threatening ruin?*

A. You are not obliged to receive her again and would act very improvidently should you ever do it. You need not maintain her.... If you cannot otherwise prevent her being trusted in business, you must cry her down publicly. Such desperate diseases must have as desperate a remedy. [Q.3, 14:24, 11 August 1694]

Q. *I have been married about eight years and by my husband's and my industry we have acquired a considerable portion of worldly goods. I have a sister in sad circumstances. I need to help maintain her family or else they could not subsist. I have a father and mother who threaten to curse me if I don't maintain them also and let my sister go a begging (I know they have enough of their own to support themselves very decently). So I desire you would be candidly pleased to give me your opinion if my parents' curse may be justly inflicted upon me.*

A. By no means. If they have a handsome subsistence, that's sufficient.... You owe respect to your father and mother, however unreasonable they may be, but you should deny them assistance if you only help them by hurting your sister. [Q.5, 16:13, 29 January 1695]

Q. *A tradesman in the country marries a gentlewoman; both pretend to great fortune, but a little time reveals them equally deceived. He goes bankrupt and is thrown into debtors' prison. She is forced to support herself and goes into service, where she lives well for several years. She has lately entered into a very good trade. Meanwhile, his creditors, being satisfied of his insolvency, discharged him from prison. He, not being used to work (having lived very well and credibly in his time), is forced to depend on her for his maintenance.*

Query: Is his wife obliged to maintain him and live with him as she did before he failed, or does she do well to keep him at a farther distance? He is scarce ever admitted to her board, although sometimes to her bed, as appears by her having lately had a child by him. Her friends think it hard she should maintain him in idleness and prompt her to severities against him and his.... Her excuse or reason why she would not live with him is because he is proud, saucy, and contentious, and that her life would be very uncomfortable. Now gentlemen, should she consider her duty or her comfort?

A. Both. Here her quiet does not contradict her duty. She having the power in her own hands may in all probability make her own conditions, which ought to be as good and honorable to such a relation as her circumstances...will admit.... She must remember he is her husband, showing her goodness and Christianity by taking some care of him who would not care for her.... We think it hard that he should want necessaries while she can supply him without injury to herself. The best method she can take is to put him in a way of business by which he may be just and honorable both to her and to those other persons he is indebted to.... We think it best for them, if possible, to live together, all past things being forgot on either side ... and he must be an ungrateful black villain that will abuse a woman that shall deal so handsomely with him. [*AO*, 2:175]

Q. *I humbly crave your speedy and best advice to the following particular. A young man married a young woman who was well descended, but fortune being not so propitious to her as to many others, ... she was left without a dowry. Her husband knew that, yet out of sincere love and affection was willing to embrace her upon honorable terms. Their marriage proved not a little distasteful to his relations, insomuch that they leave no means untried to set the young couple at variance. He does not depend for his income on his relations, but ... the consequences of their hostility I fear will prove destructive of the couple's well-being. She being virtuously inclined desires your advice on her behavior toward her husband's relations.*

A.   This is so common an error in parents that she cannot be surprised. . . . In time, by forgiving all their unhandsome reflections without seeming to resent them and respecting them . . . , she may convince them . . . that such a good and prudent wife is a much more suitable match than a golden one without these qualities. Yet if this method does not produce the wished-for effect, it will not miss its reward, since it's natural to suppose that her husband, who already loves her for her merit, will esteem her still more. . . . And should that also fail, she will have the satisfaction of mind that always results from having acted wisely and done our duty. [*AO*, 2:183–84]

Q.   *About a year and a half ago in the country I accidentally saw a young woman of wit and beauty, with whom I fell in love. Making my address to her while I stayed there for some few months, I gained her affections. When she came to town lately on business, we were privately married without the knowledge of any of her relations. But her stay here being longer than at first she designed has caused both her friends and my own to suspect what had happened (though I am sure none of them can find it out). My circumstances being at present in so poor a condition that their knowledge of it would in all probability ruin us makes me bold to desire your speedy answer to these following queries: When asked, is positively denying the marriage a sin? And if so, how shall we hide it (since its knowledge will be of so fatal consequence)?*

A.   It is not permissible to conceal any truth by telling a lie, even though revealing that truth would be prejudicial to us, for falsehood and deceit are most offensive in the sight of God Almighty. Avoid all opportunities of being asked, and likewise shun as much as possible seeing one another publicly or any action that may increase others' suspicion. If possible, carry it off with a joke, leaving everyone to their guesses. But if this won't do and you find you're likely to be discovered, report the first story yourself to a friend.... What's to be done then is only to persuade the interested relations to do that at first which they must do in the end, if they are honest people: forgive you both and make you happy as fast as they can. [*AO*, 2:530–31]

Several married men, wishing to avoid the financial burden of children, asked whether husbands and wives could cease having sexual relations. One man with an "infirm" wife was advised by a physician to travel away from home for an extended period to avoid the possibility of his wife becoming pregnant.

Q. *A young gentleman fell in love with a young lady not inferior in her fortune to his own. They married, but through some little discontent his relations took it ill. After the wedding, they blocked his inheritance. Hers being not sufficient to maintain them both equal to their former status if they have children, he ... is willing to deny himself the enjoyment of her until such time as his fortunes shall give him a better prospect of living equal to their former standing. The gentleman asks whether such a resolution be a sin?*

A. We do not believe the separation for a time (both consenting) to be a sin; but if it be continued, it is our opinion, that it is the opening for a great many sins.... It would be a dismal policy in a commonwealth that upon losses or poverty families should separate, besides the temptations that such persons are deservedly left to by God Almighty.... It's our judgment that they immediately adjust to their meaner circumstances.... Opinion and the prejudices of custom have put a very undue emphasis upon the stations of life. Industry and resignation will teach them to be happier in their present state. [Q.3, 4:8, 24 October 1691]

Q. *A person of very slender fortune and no employment ... was by the importunity of his wife about a year and a half since ... persuaded to live with her only as a brother, till I had some business whereby I might handsomely subsist.... Now the question is, do we hereby sin against the divine dictate, be fruitful and multiply?*

A.   As for what you call a divine dictate, be fruitful and multiply, we look upon abstaining to be no great contradiction to it, for that appears to be rather a declaration of our liberty to do so, as also a supposition that we are endowed with natural powers to that end. [Q.4, 8:5, 26 July 1692]

Q.   *I'm a married man ... in the flower of my strength and age, my wife infirm, and for her sake the physicians advise me to take a journey into the country to see my friends, which I find I can't do without great inconvenience. Pray your advice how I shall behave myself in this matter.*

A.   See our answer to the next question.

Q.   *I have been married some years, my wife and I middle-aged and both healthy, but never yet had any children, at which we are both extremely troubled.... My wife fancies my smoking tobacco, which I do in great quantities, may be the cause of the misfortune we both complain of.... Pray your advice in this matter.*

A.   The first querist should smoke tobacco for some time at home and not take the trip the doctor advised. If it has the effect which the wife of the second querist fancies, let him tell us, and we'll let the second one know it. [Qs. 4, 5, 10:7, 18 April 1693]

Q.   *Since the design of marriage is to propagate one's kind, why do most men regard numerous children as a curse or at least an incumbrance and great affliction? ... And is it permissible for a healthy married couple to use any means to avoid having children?*

A.   If a man has an estate and numerous children, he must live on fewer resources to provide for them. If he has none, he ought to work harder and be more diligent in his employment so he can maintain a family in future.... When children are dutiful, even if they are costly to raise, they doubly recompence the costs if their parents need help in their old age.... To the second query: Where there is a mutual consent and the health of their bodies will allow it, we believe married persons may act according to their inclinations. But if they cohabit together, no indirect means can be used to prevent having children. [Q.4, 17:28, 6 July 1695]

Q. *Can marriage and chastity consist together?*
A. Yes. Why not? A man may be temperate at the most splendid banquet and decide not to eat more than is sufficient. [*AO*, 2:254]

Numerous querists reported contentious marriages and requested advice, sometimes mentioning the possibility of separation or divorce. The Athenians occasionally responded with jokes when men described their desire to control misbehaving wives, displaying a misogynistic attitude usually absent from their other answers.

Q. *How shall a woman that is plagued with an ill husband reclaim or make him better?*
A. Show him this *Mercury*, and tell him . . . his name shall be printed in it at length the first Tuesday of the next month. But the best direction that can be given . . . is to be as patient as possible unless the husband is such a brute that this manner of behavior will make him more insulting. [Q.2, 3:4, 8 August 1691]

Q. *How may a man reclaim a headstrong or unruly wife?*
A. Give her rope enough—Our meaning is, let her alone.... But the surest way of all is being a good husband yourself, for bad husbands are very often the cause that wives are no better. [Q.1, 3:13, 8 September 1691]

Q. *May a lady having a man to her husband that keeps ill company and debauches himself with common whores break the bond of marriage by separating herself from him and marrying again or by repaying him in his own coin?*

A. Upon proof of adultery, she may sue out a divorce from bed and board and one third of the effects of the estate for maintenance, but the law allows not a second marriage while he is living. As for falseness to him in revenge, it is very wicked and ridiculous, because the person that transgresses injures him (or her) self more than the other. [Q.4, 3:21, undated, after 26 September 1691]

Q. *I am married to a man by the law of the land, but not I think by the laws of God and nature. He is so rigid as to abuse and beat me and is also guilty of all manner of debauchery. Query: Is it sin for me to leave him?*

A. Upon a supposition of abuses, debauchery, etc., the last, if proved to be matter of fact, is sufficient cause to be divorced from bed and board, but the law allows no second marriages while either party lives. [Q.6, 3:25, undated, after 26 September 1691]

Q. *A person has a perverse, contentious wife. Is it lawful for him, she also consenting (sincerely to avoid passion and contention, since very destructive to his inward peace and his duty), to separate and live asunder?*

A. If the querist is unhappy in a perverse wife, it's more than probable he would be more unhappy without her.... They may separate for a time (both consenting), but it must be for fasting and prayer, and then come together again, lest Satan tempt them to incontinence. [Q.7, 4:2, 3 October 1691]

Q. *Gentlemen, I have the ill fortune to be married to a man whose extravagance is such that I am reduced to a miserable condition. He has for some years ... neglected his trade and spent his money and time ... in the company of lewd women, causelessly leaving his family to want bread, as we have often done.... He will often flaunt his relationships with whores in front of me.... He now talks of selling his goods, and so to leave me.... And now my request to you is whether I were not better to take away such of the goods as may be of use for me and my child in his absence, and go from him.... Or what other advice can you give a miserable woman, almost distracted with the cruel dealings of an untoward husband?*

A. If true, this is a miserable story, yet common. Still, when women in such conditions are advised to redress themselves and their children by applying to the parish for assistance, they would rather complain and take pride in complaining than seek such aid. This circumstance helps to create ill husbands. [Q.9, 9:24, 4 March 1693]

Q. *I've a dreadful scold of a wife and would willingly give you half my estate if you could tell me how to tame her.*

A. The method we'd prescribe for taming your shrew is to laugh at her and let her scold on until she is weary. Seem to take no notice of her.... Say nothing to her, unless a little by the by. Ten to one when she sees herself slighted, she'll burst from mere vexation. [Q.6, 10:8, 22 April 1693]

Q. *I'm a tradesman.... I follow my business and ... procure a competent maintenance for my family.... Yet I have the misfortune of having a wife that will often upbraid me.... Now I desire to know whether ... I may beat her in order to bring her to a more prudent behavior.*

A. Beat her! No sir! By no means.... Get a pretty little padlock for her tongue, ... or ... draw a tooth once a day, or after every lecture; or lastly, procure a preferment for her in Bedlam, and then you may promise yourself a little quiet. [Q.2, 10:25, 20 June 1693]

Q. *Gentlemen, I kept a coffeehouse and made a livelihood by it, but my wife used to go to a tavern in an evening or to gentlemen's chambers in a morning to drink, as I was made to believe, for the love of wine only. . . . I was advised by some friends to keep wine myself to take away her pretensions, by which I find a very comfortable profit. But my wife being educated in a tavern and naturally inclined to wine and company-keeping of all sorts . . . puts evil thoughts into my mind and makes my head often to ache. My neighbors point their fingers at me. Now if I stop selling wine, I lose a certain profit, and if I continue it, she is exposed in her reputation, loses her health, and in the long run maybe her precious soul into the bargain. . . . What course shall I take to preserve my trade and my wife's health and reputation, my own quiet, and still keep the wine trade going?*

A. Truly, honest friend, if your wife will be drunk, etc., it's best and most private at home, . . . but this supposes that you can be content with cuckoldry. If you will take our opinion in the case, take your opportunity for witnesses, and get a divorce from her, for if she is irrecoverably gone for drinking and cheating, it's scandal, unhappiness, and sin to have any involvement at all with her. [Q3, 11:6, 29 July 1693]

Q. *A young gentleman, aged twenty-one and without a fortune, married an old woman nearly fifty years old with a bad reputation . . . because of his eager desire for her fortune. Since marriage she has shown that she deserved her poor reputation by proving a bitter and virulent scold, alienating part of her fortune and disposing it among her children. She has also contracted a great many debts, which she has left him to pay, even though there is little left to pay them with. . . . Still worse, she has defamed him and is ruining his reputation, dearer to him than his life. . . .*

He wants to part from her and to live separately. . . . Several people have convinced him of her former lewdness (which he did not believe before marriage). . . . She has given no sign of a reformation . . . and he is confirmed she was very wanton in her youth. Your opinion is desired if he should still live . . . with a woman he has a

very bad opinion of. Or may he with a good conscience live sepa-
rately from her, though he never found her in the act of adultery?

A.   Poor unhappy youth! We see no remedy to his misfortune
without mutual consent. Then if they can both live honestly, we believe they may part.... He should have investi-
gated her former course of life before marriage.... If it can
be had, quietness together is to be preferred to their living
asunder. To achieve that he must never reproach her with
what is past, but be sure to give her no cause for anger. If her
behavior remains the same, we believe that he may leave
her if she'll agree to it. Otherwise, he can't. [Q.2, 17:26, 29
June 1695]

Q.   *What method shall the woman take who is married to the most*
vexatious, sordid, malicious, proud, insolent, conceited, covetous,
jealous, cross, crabbed, merciless, cruel, contentious, forward, per-
verse wretch in the world?... Why obey your husband when he is
so far from loving his wife that he hates her? Nor is he capable of
loving anything but a pipe of tobacco and gaming.... His wife has
always been faithful to him, careful of his business, and brought
him a fortune above his circumstances or merit.... She can have
no manner of comfort in association with him. May she therefore
have liberty to divert herself with civil company provided there be
no breach of virtue? She does not plan to be in any man's company
alone. She would only like to converse a little more with others to
lighten the unbearable yoke that she's compelled to bear during
her lifetime, unless God is merciful and takes him away by death,
which she still hopes might happen.

A.   Surely the poor man who has all these hard words thrown
at him would have a response to each.... But supposing
all these ill words are true of the man and all the good of
the woman,... that he really behaves himself as here represented, and that she has given him no provocation,...
the method she's to take is the same she would under the
plague or any other terrible and unavoidable calamity. She

must submit to God's will and bear every burden patiently, waiting for God to deliver her.... Unless he's false to her bed or threatens her life, she can't honestly leave him.... She needs to be careful what company she keeps when not with him. Also she must not neglect her family or him, since there's a great deal of danger that she might not long continue to be the faithful, careful wife that she's now described. [Q.1, 19:6, 15 November 1695]

Q. *Pray which is the greater fault, for an undutiful wife to say that her husband has beaten her when he has not, or for the husband to beat such a wife? What punishment is fit for such a husband and such a wife?*

A. Beating is so very bad a remedy that it's as bad as the disease itself.... We scarce know which is worse.... If it be asked what punishment is fit for such a husband and such a wife, we reply that the most proper punishment for them in our opinion is that they should still live together and plague one another. [Q.3, 19:24, 18 January 1696]

Q. *What shall be done to the wife who calls her husband coward and tells him she can beat him if she wants to if he ever strikes her? And says she will complain about him to a justice of the peace, when he never struck her or so much as threatened her?*

A. For the first, if she gives you ill language, stop her mouth with a kiss and show her you are no coward by not being conquered by a woman's anger. If you can kiss her whether she will agree or not, it will be a convincing argument that you are still the stronger and would prevent her from going to the justice of the peace.... But if she has been there already and sworn falsely against you, the best way to be revenged on her is to treat her so kindly in the future that if she should swear the peace against you a hundred times, nobody will believe her. [Q.3{4}, 19:24, 18 January 1696]

Q. *I have been married to a man a few years who has much deceived me in my expectations as to his good husbandry and love. Lacking an estate of his own, he spends extravagantly and wholly depends on my industry for his maintenance. Besides, he keeps company with other women and a child (now dead) was laid to him about a year ago. Although he denies it, by circumstances and the woman's oath all his friends are satisfied it's true. He has since frequented some other women who have given him worse than a child.*

All of this has caused me to resolve never to live with him again as my husband, but he has now got well again. He solicits me himself and through his friends to waive my resolve and live together as man and wife, promising a thorough reformation. I desire to know which is the least evil: to break my protestation and vow to God Almighty and live with him again as before or leave him to his ruin by my unkindness, as he calls it.

A. The vow you made was because of his lewdness and on supposition of his persisting in it and made to prevent your own ruin. If therefore he really reforms, we think the reason for your vow ceasing, the obligation of it ceases too. Being the wronged person, you are at liberty to forgive him or not, as shall appear to you most prudent and convenient. If you take our advice, he should keep a long Lent first before you again trust him, to see whether his reformation were real or only a pretense to delude you and once more endanger your ruin. [*AO*, 2:125–26]

Some correspondents revealed the existence of multiple spouses or prospects of such, displaying an indifference to matrimonial legalities.

Q. *If polygamy were allowed, would we have a more temperate age than now we have?*

A. Much otherwise, from the very thing itself; for certainly... he's a more temperate man that can dine upon one dish, than he that gorges himself upon twenty or thirty.... The drunkard is ever dry, . . . and the more wealth a covetous man has, the more still he scrapes for. And this we learn from experience as well as reason—Where are fouler lusts than in those countries where polygamy is allowed, particularly in the Turkish seraglios and all the Eastern nations? [Q.4, 3:4, 8 August 1691]

Q. *Suppose a young man, not concerned therein, should out of curiosity show his mistress the query about polygamy in your* Athenian Mercury, *Vol. 3, Number 4, and she thereupon rejects him. What in this case would be the greater, his folly or her severity?*

A. We should be heartily sorry if our *Mercury* should be so much as the innocent cause of any man's misfortune. . . . Accordingly, we must here be forced to give the decision against the lady, to whom the gentleman might with the greatest innocence in the world show that or any other question and desire her opinion thereof. And if she does not again entertain him, we pronounce her in the name of all our society faithless and foolish, and unworthy the honor and happiness of a constant lover. [Q.7, 3:15, 15 September 1691]

Q. *I having spent some of my estate was forced to take an employment under the king, which caused me to leave my family. I being placed in a town, . . . one of the young ladies fell in love with me. . . . I told her I was married and had several children, but she importuned me to marry her if my wife should die. . . . I promised . . . and after 4 months' time I was removed to another place.*

   Being there about one month, a widow about 40 years old fell in love with me. . . . This widow never had any children and has at her own disposal 150£ per annum, the other has but 60£ per annum. I having promised both, I desire your answer in your next, which I ought to have when my wife dies.

A. If you will forecast the future in this way, think what a choice your wife (that you now have) ought to make, amongst the

numerous suitors which she will have when you are dead.
[Q.4, 10:18, 27 May 1693]

Q. *A young gentlewoman being some time since by the consent of her
friends married to a gentleman, lived a little while very comfortably with him. But making a discovery that he was married to
another at the same time he courted her, she absented herself from
him and returned to her friends. She is now courted by another to
a second marriage, which she refuses, thinking her obligation to her
husband makes it unlawful. Your opinion is desired: Because she
was altogether ignorant of his first marriage when he courted her,
may she embrace this offer of a second husband though her first is
yet alive? It is also thought that he has married a third time since
she left him.*

A. Your marriage to this great Turk of a husband that keeps such
a seraglio of women must be void, because by our laws a
man can have but one wife at one time, nor (we think) does
the Christian law allow any more. Consequently, you are
not in bondage in that case but may embrace any fair offer
that's made you, although you ought not to impose on your
new servant, but let him know what sort of a widow you
are, if he's yet ignorant of it. [Q.4, 11:11, 15 August 1693]

Q. *A man had two wives and died. He owed me some money and paid
me 16£ more than he owed. Now I desire to know, which of them
has a right to it?*

A. Only the first was his wife. Therefore, if he disposed of it
to nobody else, it belongs only to her. [Q.3, 11:17, 5 September 1693]

Q. *A gentleman's wife left him more than seven years ago. He thinks it is
now lawful and needful to marry and live honestly. At present he
makes honorable love to a gentlewoman who has a good fortune.
She is a modest woman and is loath to take a chance on him,
although she's inclined very much to love him. But he has had*

relationships with other men's wives. He is a man of quality or
pretends to be. Your advice is speedily desired.

A. And let it be as speedy as it will, ten to one our advice will
    come too late. We can only say, if the lady be as wise as the
    querist affirms her to be modest, she'll not long deliberate
    what she ought to do, nor any longer question whether
    she ought to reject a confessed notorious adulterer. That's
    the only quality, it seems, that she's certain of. [Q.3, 14:6, 9
    June 1694]

Q. *About five years ago my daughter married a man who by all accounts*
    seems to be incapable of fathering children. They enjoy a plentiful
    estate and may expect a larger one in the future. I desire to know
    whether she may lawfully with the consent of her husband choose
    some other man to procure an heir?

A. If it appears plain that the fault is his, she may be divorced. But
    she cannot so innocently admit another to her bed while
    she is his supposed wife as she might have done before she
    was married. . . . Besides, if the design proves successful,
    their guilt would be increased by bringing a false heir into
    the family, since that would cheat some other person of
    his right to the property. A true heir is supposed to be his
    as well as hers. [Q.6, 14:7, 12 June 1694]

Q. *Does that passage of St. Paul in 1 Timothy 3:2—A bishop must be*
    the husband of one wife—seem to allow that the apostle permit-
    ted other men to have additional wives? I cannot decide how to
    interpret it. . . . I judge myself brisk and amorous. I hate whoring,
    but I would think polygamy the happiest life in the world were it
    not forbidden. . . . I am at last resolved to be determined by you.

A. The reason we have so many unhappy marriages is because
    the generality of the world are incapable of knowing what
    true love is, but instead like you have such an unreason-
    able and unruly passion to be satisfied. . . . They seek a fair
    face or a diversity of such rather than a wise woman and

a friend, but the outcome generally shows the misfortune of the choice. The conversation of one ingenious woman who is wise enough to love and prudent and agreeable in temperament will give more felicity ... than a thousand women. . . . True love is only between two, and without that all the pleasures of life are insipid. This was shown by our wise creator, who at first made but two people, as a full complement of each other's happiness. [Q.1, 14:11, 26 June 1694]

Q. *A virtuous man married a wife in part to live honestly. After some years together with several children born and yet living, she has forsaken him and obstinately refuses to live with him or so much as to see him. He's under great temptation to that sin which he married to avoid, which he now in vain endeavors to overcome.... He desires your judgment if with his wife continuing so obstinate and refusing his company without any cause, he can take another in her place or what means he ought to take to reclaim her.*

A. It's strange she should thus forsake him without any cause. If he has been guilty of either falsehood or unkindness, he ought to do all he can to recompense and reconcile with her. If he has been both faithful and obliging and has taken care to provide for her, one would think it should not be so difficult to reconcile them by the means of a common friend. If she's a person of piety or virtue, she should consider that nothing can warrant such separation other than a notorious breach of the marriage vow by her husband or his absolute neglect of providing for her. Consequently, she's guilty of a great sin for forsaking him ... and exposing him to such temptations as she knows she does. . . .

As for him, he can't be at liberty to marry another, unless he can get a divorce from her with approval for a new marriage from the supreme judicial authority of this nation. If he cannot do that nor reconcile with his wife, he has no option but frequent fasting and mortification, along with such honest and prudent methods that he would have used had he never married. Those must have the good effects he desires though with some difficulty, for we should never have been commanded to live honestly had there not been a possibility of doing so. [Q.1, 18:1, 16 July 1695]

Q. *A woman left her husband, married another, and, after his death, a third, at which she's now troubled. Query: Should she live with the third as her husband?*

A. Not unless she's sure her former husband is dead, unless she'll venture to live in continued adultery. [*AO*, 2:95–96]

Q. *I was married more than a year ago to a young woman with a fortune suitable to my own and have so far lived very comfortably with her. But now a man of a much meaner fortune than either of ours says he was married to her three years ago, even though she's only sixteen and a half. His account is not denied by her or her father, but they say the marriage was not consummated, and they gave the fellow a piece of money to leave her. He went to sea, but now he's returned and claims her as his wife. I'm a tradesman and extremely troubled lest this situation, if known, should blast my reputation. I desire your advice in this case. Whose wife is she and what should I do in so intricate a matter?*

A. We think it undeniable that she was an infant when thirteen. Therefore, she was not capable of disposing of herself, especially against the consent of her father, as she seems to have done. Along with its not being consummated, that makes the former, we think, no marriage. However, there might be the inconvenience of a lawsuit in the case, and the noise of the thing, which the querist is justly afraid of. For those reasons he must take the same way the father did before (though it was not very honest in him to let the querist know nothing about it), and give the "half-husband" another piece of money and let him totally resign what we think is none of his. [*AO*, 2:169]

And finally...

Q. *About twelve years ago a tradesman in this town who was newly set up in business married a young woman who was about seventeen years of age. Her relations were dead; her fortunes were 600£, which was paid him on the day of marriage. The woman quickly found that her husband neglected his trade, which made her more careful to get an insight into it herself. Being a quick and industrious woman, in a little time she understood and managed the trade as well as any man could do. Thus, for eight years they lived together... and had six children, three of whom are still living.*

He since that time is fallen to gaming, drinking, etc.... They have not for these four years lain in bed together, which nobody knew until he told one of his neighbors, to whom he also declared that for these two years he has not been capable of lying with any woman. This neighbor of his is a single man, has a free estate of 300£ per annum, and has made this proposal to the other... that he (the single man) would take her to him as his wife, that he would be bound to maintain the three children,... that he will settle on her 100£ a year,... and that he will allow him the said husband 20£ a year for his maintenance.

The man... was overjoyed at his good fortune. Away they both went to the woman and told her what they had agreed on if she would consent... but she obstinately refuses, saying that she thinks it is adultery so to do. Now is it not the same thing in the sight of God... as though her husband were really dead, since in the first place he never took care for her maintenance and since he has not for these two years been capable of performing matrimonial duties? I'll assure you the whole relation is true.

A. We could heartily wish the relation were not true.... The unhappy, good-natured woman ... does certainly deserve better than to be brought into further unhappiness. If the proposers object that the law itself allows divorces, we answer that it does so. Both the law of God and the law of this land make adultery to be a sufficient reason.... Divorce may be from bed and board, but second marriages are not allowed. . . .

Perhaps no history or records will afford an example so full of folly, disgrace, unkindness, and ridicule as this. But to the particulars of the question, whether non-maintenance, etc. render her husband dead in the sight of God, we answer no, . . . for we have not one precedent for it either in law, history, or divinity. [no Q number, 3:19, undated, after 26 September 1691]

CHAPTER 6

"A Very Amorous Disposition"

DANGEROUS LIAISONS

CORRESPONDENTS FREQUENTLY ASKED THE Athenians about sexual behavior outside of marriage—both premarital and adulterous. Commonly, querists themselves were involved in such relationships and perhaps sought advice on ending them. But not always: cloaked in anonymity, questioners could reveal their deepest sexual secrets to the Athenians, who usually replied with censure for past faults along with encouragement for future reformation.

The Athenians responded to general questions about sexuality and sexual misbehavior as well as to specific ones.

Q. *Why are common women seldom or never with child?*
A. Why does not the grass grow in the pathway? [Q.10, 1:18, 23 May 1691]

Q. *In a dishonorable amour, who is most to blame, the man in tempting or the woman in yielding?*
A. We think the man...because he's the very cause of the evil. The woman had been virtuous had he not tempted her. [Q.11, 3:4, 8 August 1691]

Q. *Is it possible for one woman to love another as passionately and constantly as if the love were between different sexes?*

A. As constantly they soon may, but as passionately how should they, unless they are a man turned into a woman? [Q.3, 11:25, 3 October 1693]

Q. *If men were equally punished with women for deluding women or maids in the streets or other places, would it be a good law and possibly put a stop to the debauchery of the city?*
A. Aye, and of the kingdom, too, if you could get it passed. [Q.12, 12:15, 12 December 1693]

Q. *There are two ladies in love with me to the degree that nothing will satisfy them but marrying me. They both are content to take each other as a partner rather than lose me, yet fearing it's a sin, we know not what to do but will await your advice.*
A. It's a hundred to one that you will not be liked as well after marriage as before, and it's probable you won't much like the prohibition of one woman or the other. Therefore, you'd better try them out first and afterward let her take you that likes you best. [Q.3, 15:19, 9 November 1694]

Q. *Pray what considerations are proper and useful when a man is beset with temptations? How shall he excite his reason or behave himself to avoid or prevail against sins that are frequently committed against the dictates of conscience, such as fornication and the like?*
A. Reason is not enough. There must be faith, too, to subdue this traitor within us as well as the devil, our declared and open enemy. We mean faith in the largest extent of the word, an actual lively belief of what God has revealed, especially the rewards and punishments of another life and of his own presence everywhere and consciousness of all our actions.... We need to fly from this as we would from any other less formidable danger and avoid all occasions and temptations leading to sin, as well as to sloth, intemperance, and the like. Add fasting and other acts of mortification to these methods where necessary, as St. Paul

did himself in order to subdue the rebel within. [Q.5, 19:9, 26 November 1695]

Three generally phrased questions nevertheless seemed specific enough to refer to particular cases. Every reader would have understood what the second querist meant by "too well acquainted"; similar phrases appeared in other questions and answers.

Q. *Does he who solicits his neighbor's wife on behalf of another amply prove himself both friend and pimp?*

A. Undoubtedly a pimp and such a friend as the devil may be said to be. That is no act of friendship, for the very essence of friendship consists of virtuous actions. [Q.2, 12:19, 26 December 1693]

Q. *Should two persons of different sexes marry, if they have been too well acquainted?*

A. They have more right to one another than anybody else, especially if a child is involved and there's any likelihood they'll both live more honestly afterward. [Q.4, 15:27, 4 December 1694]

Q. *Is it permissible for a man whose circumstances are very unhappy and hinder him from marriage to castrate himself in order to deliver himself from the most urgent temptations? ... And as for the objection that the operation may endanger life, that is slight, for if it is done by a good surgeon, the danger is little or none.*

A. It is the same in effect whether a man is a eunuch or resolves to deny himself the embraces of a woman, which ... some have wholly relinquished so that they might be the more disengaged from the world and devote themselves to piety. It is doubtful whether castration would remove all such unruly desires, but if we were assured it would ... yet though done by the best surgeon, it cannot be permitted since the outcome is uncertain. [Q.1, 18:9, 13 August 1695]

Two men wrote to ask advice about ending their practice of masturbation, also in terms that everyone at the time would have understood, although they referred to "sin" or "vice." The second question hinted at some sort of group activity.

Q. *I have formerly addicted myself to a most grievous sin, and though I have for some considerable time (by the grace of God) refrained from the commission of it . . . yet notwithstanding in my dreams I seem to commit it and to take a pleasure in the commission of it. I desire you would give me your opinion; do I yet sin or not?*

A. Involuntary Motions are not wicked, because not to be avoided, and what cannot be avoided is no sin. . . . Other persons have experienced the very same circumstances. [no Q number, 3:20, after 27 September 1691]

Q. *I am a young man and very much addicted to a vice which I assuredly know to be a great offense against God. . . . I made a vow not to commit the said sin until such a time was expired in hopes by such a course I should in time stop it. But before the time expired, I happened to see others committing the said sin, at which time I unhappily, though much against my will, did commit it, though I had no inclination to it. Query: By this have I broken my vow, and what ought I to do for the future to keep it better?*

A. First, you did ill to promise not to commit it until such a time, whereas you should have resolved the same for your entire lifetime. By God's grace, that certainly was in your power as to this particular sin. . . . Example can never require behavior though it may strongly incline either to good or evil. . . . Whence it follows that you have as much broken your vow as he who commits adultery has broken the Seventh Commandment. Our advice on the whole is that you heartily ask God Almighty's pardon for it, resolving by his grace never more to commit it; and that you devoutly and constantly attend the public service if possible every weekday and at least twice every Sunday. You should also receive the holy sacrament weekly, not neglecting constant private prayer each morning and evening. Those are the best means (and we think infallible) to quiet your mind and to guard you for the future against the same temptation. [Q.5, 11:28, 14 October 1693]

One querist's language was so general as to make definitive interpretation of the sexual misbehavior impossible, although he or she probably referred to an illicit heterosexual relationship.

Q. *It has been my misfortune to be seduced into a very great sin and not only so, but to make the most solemn oaths and promises to continue in it. If I break them, I'm perjured; if I continue in it, I'm in as ill a condition. Pray your advice what way to take in it.*

A. A promise, oath, or obligation to do an ill thing is not binding. It's not only false words but ill actions that are lies, being deviations from truth or equity. To vow to do an ill thing and perform it is a greater complication of guilt, ... but by breaking such a wicked oath you honor the truth. [Q.8, 4:7, 20 October 1691]

Heterosexual relationships almost inevitably produced inquiries involving pregnancy and paternity. The first question below was the very first personal query the Athenians answered in spring 1691. In its initial form, the question made clear that the correspondent was asking on his own behalf, not for "a friend," a later alteration. The Athenians' response was consistent with sexual belief at the time, which held that a woman had to experience orgasm to become pregnant. In their answer to the first part of the second example, the Athenians displayed a dry wit occasionally evident in other replies as well.

Q. *A friend of mine is like to have a child fathered on him. The mother confesses he never lay with her but once and then she was a maid. Query: Is it possible to lose a maidenhead and conceive a child at the same time?*

A. Naturalists tell us (and offer examples) that great falls and extreme coughs are sometimes so violent as to break the hymen ... but such accidents are rare. ... A maid the first time undergoes too much of the rack and torture to be capable of acting her part effectually. In addition, a young man's eagerness pushes him to do what is natural for him to do before the critical time. No physician will be so uncharitable as not to allow a possibility of an act of this nature, yet most would place it amongst those things that are next to impossibilities, especially in an age which produces a sex more delicate and tender than ordinary. ... I would almost as soon believe the relation of Averroes, concerning the woman that conceived in a bath by attracting the seminal effluxion of a man admitted to bathe near her. [Q.10, 1, undated issue, spring 1691]

Q. *Gentlemen, I am a young gentlewoman in the very prime of my youth, and if my glass flatters me not, tolerable handsome, likewise co-heiress of a very fair estate. My sister and I will enjoy what my aged father's many years' industry has acquired. Though my father has ever shown himself lovingly tender, . . . he often has assured us that nothing should so soon quench the flame of his paternal love as our deviation from the strict rules of pure chastity and its handmaid, modesty. Now to my utter ruin and eternal shame (if anything unknowingly committed may be termed shameful), I am with child. How, when, where, and by whom to my greatest grief I know not. But this, alas, I know too well, that the hour wherein my father hears of it, I am disinherited of his estate, banished his love, etc. Gentlemen, I earnestly implore you to give me some relief by resolving these two queries:*

1. *Is it possible for a woman to carnally know a man in her sleep so as to conceive, for I am sure in this and no other way was I got with child?*

2. *Is it permissible to use means to put a stop to this growing mischief and kill it in the embryo, this being the only way to avert the thunderclap of my father's indignation?*

A. To the first question, Madam, we are very positive that you are luckily mistaken, for the thing is absolutely impossible if you know nothing of it.... So that you may set your heart at rest and think no more of the matter. As for the second question, such practices are murder, and those that are so unhappy as to ... use the forementioned means will certainly one day find the remedy worse than the disease. There are wiser methods to be taken in such cases, such as a small journey and a confidant. And afterward such a pious and good life as may redress such a heavy misfortune. [Q.2, 11:4, 22 July 1693] [*AO*, 2:240]

Q. *Some time ago a servant maid was got with child in her master's house. After she was delivered, she went voluntarily before a justice of the peace and swore that her master was the father of the child. Therefore, he was bound over for legal proceedings at the next court. Two weeks later, the master took the wench before another justice. Then she swore she was persuaded to swear the child was her master's but that the apprentice was the father. So there are two fathers. The question is: Which is the right one, and how can the wench's oath be believed, for it is plain she has perjured herself regardless of who is the father?*

A. Here's a case beyond the facts and the law, which needs almost another Solomon to decide it.... Here are two fathers and yet they won't own one poor bastard between them.... It seems hard on the poor child.... For an obvious reason, the mother may not well know which is the father.... There can be no dependence on her oath.... We know not how to proceed to judgment without further evidence. We suppose that the parties concerned would be well pleased if the parish would take responsibility for the child ... but we know no remedy other than both fathers should maintain it betwixt them. [Q.7, 15:4, 15 September 1694]

One man told the woman he was courting about his sexual conquests; she asked the Athenians for their opinion.

Q. *A lady has received the private addresses of a gentleman for almost seven years. His fortune is so small that he dares make no public statements of affection lest they should be frustrated by her friends. He has always behaved himself toward her with that honor and respect due to her birth and virtue and pretends to be most passionately and unfeignedly in love with her. He makes her his confidant in all the secret affairs of his life, among the rest giving her a particular account of several women he has very often lain with since he courted her.*

    Your opinion is desired: Can anyone violently in love be guilty of such actions? Or should she expect him to behave the same way after marriage as he does before? Or should she esteem him for his sincerity in telling her what he might so easily keep secret from her and marry him on promise of constancy for the future?

A. Pray, Madam, let's first ask you some questions before we resolve yours. Does your ladyship think your spark would admire your ladyship more and believe your promises to be constant after marriage if you yourself admitted to the embraces of such and such gallants? Then told him about it out of pure love and sincerity and as soon as you came together resolve to stop it? If you think he would not be pleased with it, why should you be pleased with the same? It's plain you are yet seeking marriage, and people are seldom more inclined to constancy after marriage than before. It's plain he thinks you are not virtuous or would make you lose your virtue, and for that reason he gives you examples of others. [Q.6, 12:24, 12 January 1694]

Three young women wrote to ask the Athenians' advice about how to deal with suitors whom they feared would entice them into sexual misconduct. The Athenians confirmed their correspondents' fears and advised them to leave the relationships.

Q. *A gentleman that has been married for several years has lately fallen in love with a young gentlewoman so passionately that he says it's death for him not to see her, although he protests he'd rather die than offer any injury to her virtue. However, she thinks it not a good idea to keep him company and desires your thoughts and advice upon it.*

A. He may fall in lust, but in love he cannot, being himself married. Every look with such an irregular desire is in our Savior's opinion a virtual adultery. His protesting he'd rather die than affront her is the usual cant of those who pursue such designs. . . . Our advice therefore is to all that are in such circumstances and temptations to stop their ears and eyes against these he-sirens, and never to admit any conversation with them as they value reputation or heaven. [Q.2, 13:19, 10 April 1694]

Q. *About four years ago I was staying with a family and one of the sons addressed himself to me. I told him his parents would not like it, for my fortune was much inferior to his, and that I feared he would incur his father's displeasure. He said he loved no woman on earth but me. . . . All his actions persuaded me his intentions were real. . . . I love him not for his estate, for if he did not have six pence in the world I would love him as I do. . . . We made a mutual vow and called God to witness. . . . He is twelve years older than I. He is a scholar. . . .*

But before I left that family's house I was told he was married to a gentlewoman who had borne his child. I told him the story; he protested that it was false and that the child was not his. . . . He invited me recently to see his house, where I observed some goods marked with the gentlewoman's name. That made me very uneasy. . . . I have since found a letter that when I read I almost died. . . . She tells him she loves him more than her life and signs herself thus, "no more at present from your truest of lovers." . . . Gentlemen, pray, as soon as you possibly can, advise me in this matter, for there's no one else who knows this story, nor can I confide in any other person to ask their advice.

A. We'd not willingly either injure an innocent gentleman nor mislead you who desire our advice, but if the letter you

found was worded as you relate ... the writer of it must at
least be more than an ordinary friend or acquaintance. And
he is a very bad man to endeavor to deceive you both. We
think that his behavior should go a long way toward remov-
ing your love from him and settling it on a more worthy
object who neither will nor can deceive or abuse you. [Q.8,
14:23, 7 August 1694]

Q. *A gentleman pretends great kindness to me and has promised that
he'll marry me after an old woman has died, for he expects to be
her heir. He says he fears she will never give her consent for him
to marry me, because I am so unequal to him as to fortune. He
would have had me break a piece of silver with him as a token of
fidelity, but he did not want any friend of mine to be a witness.
If I consent to this, I'm sure he'd expect some greater favor than
I should be willing to grant before marriage. I have promised to
submit to your judgment. May two persons (being just to one
another and designing really to marry when their circumstances
will permit) lie together before marriage without a breach of
God's law?*

A. As we have said before, we don't expect that any of these sort
of querists will have patience or honesty enough to wait for
our answer.... She is not it seems at all concerned at the
infamy which has been justly laid on concubinage without
marriage, nor the particular laws of her own nation, nor the
usages of her church.... One would think the illegitimacy
of her children would have some little influence on her
mind.... Has she any security that her spark will be true
after all and won't turn her out to care for herself when he
has taken from her of all he cares for? ... If women generally think their lot is hard by reason of their subjection to
their husbands' despotic power, how much harder must be
theirs who depend for their bread on the lust of any man,
his absolute will and pleasure, and the ebbs and flows of

his fancy?...And can there be a more vehement suspicion of anything than that this wonderfully virtuous spark will never marry her when he...confesses his intentions by refusing to let her have any witness to the contract between them? [Q.I, 18:30, 26 October 1695]

Questions often came from people who had already engaged in premarital sex, not simply from those who were solicited for such activity. The Athenians showed little patience for or tolerance of correspondents who admitted such behavior. Still, they advised confessions only to God. The first answer below left readers to fill in the blanks.

Q. *A lady of good birth and fortune has granted some private favors to me, but at the same time so discreetly as to preserve her reputation. A friend of mine courts her honorably and desires me to tell him unfeignedly my opinion of her virtue. Query: How shall I behave myself in this case so as not to transgress the rules of honor nor friendship?*

A. If by that expression, "some private favors," be meant what everyone will suspect that reads the question, all the answer we'll give is: marry her quickly yourself, for until that's done, whatever fine names you put upon the matter, you're a ____ and she's a ____. [Q.8, 3:4, 8 August 1691]

Q. *A young man of a very amorous disposition has had the misfortune to yield to every attack of his passion.... He has promised two young gentlewomen marriage and therefore enjoyed them both. This heat of imprudent love being over, he is very sensible of his fault and very melancholy upon it. His inclinations do not lead him to have either of them,... nor can he see any means to make her or them a satisfactory restitution. I therefore beg your best advice.*

A. First let him heartily beg pardon of God Almighty and continue the same every day he lives. Then, unless there be any private reason, or rather necessity, why he should marry one more than the other (and there can be but one, which he may easily guess), we think he ought to marry neither.... If they both live and refuse to release him, he must remain single all his life, since he cannot lawfully marry either of them or any other. [Q.4, 5:13, 12 January 1692]

Q.   *I am almost 33 and have for the past 15 years led an idle and loose life. I ... regret that I wasted so many years in debauchery and extravagance. I want to reform, but I have repeatedly acted badly. When I was about 18, I swore falsely to an account for financial gain. Some years later, I swore to a young woman's mother ... that I would marry her. Soon after I nevertheless courted a virtuous lady with a good estate and ... we made a mutual promise, but she ... put me off for some years. At length I grew tired and withdrew my affections, placing them on another woman (who was then a wife). The virtuous lady then ... married another. The husband of my new lady died suddenly, which allowed me to renew my addresses, less than honorably. I have promised her marriage but have not yet performed it. This woman has no fortune, and I have wasted mine. I have two older sisters whose portions I have consumed. They are both unmarried and depend upon me. I am in debt and have no employment nor income. I run further into debt and my sisters have to work for their living. I have behaved myself so foolishly that I have neither relation nor acquaintance that will do anything for me.*

Gentlemen, I humbly beg you to direct which way I shall make my peace with God and man.... Queries: Did I commit perjury when I swore that oath to the account? Was my oath to the mother of the first woman binding? Was I guilty of breach of promise to the second and am I obliged to marry the third? Or may I marry another who will enable me to pay my debts and make restitution to my sisters? ... Can I receive the sacrament in my current state, I mean with an unfeigned repentance of my past sins? ... Gentlemen, I do humbly desire your advice and am resolved to follow your directions.

A. As to the matter of accounts…if you did not injure anybody, your sin was only against God Almighty and must be confessed to him. If you did injure anyone, you ought to make restitution or resolve to do so as soon as you can. As for your oath to the mother of the first woman, it was…no contract with the daughter. When the daughter contracted with another, your obligation ceased. As for your promise to the second, your sin was…living so ill as to discourage her from marrying you.…As for your obligations to the third lady, if you enjoyed her upon condition of marriage you ought to marry her publicly despite the financial consequences. But if not, it's our opinion that you are free, for marriage is a sacred institution. Its ends are poorly achieved by tying oneself to an adulteress, or at least one who has not given very good evidence of repentance for being so. As to your marrying a fourth, it depends upon your management of the third and what has passed between you, which you have not described sufficiently to us, so we ask you to consult a learned clergyman.…As for your repentance, you ought to be as particular and resolved as you can before you take the sacrament, and you should have a particular spiritual guide to always be ready at hand to consult upon occasion. [Q.4, 8:7, 20 September 1692]

Q. *I am a very young woman, of some quality and very pretty.…A certain lewd and infamous disturber of my honor…has, to be plain, been a little too busy where he had nothing to do. But I have since had the good fortune to enter matrimony, … and I managed all things so that my husband knew nothing of the matter. However, I'm since my marriage extremely troubled for the cheat I've put upon him and the injury I conceive I have done him, which has so afflicted my mind that my body sympathizes with it. I'm worn away to a mere skeleton.… Your advice?*

A. Why did you marry him, which you ought not in strict virtue and honor to have done? … You ought to have been the wife of your first acquaintance or else always to have lived unmarried. We think you are however ... not obliged to accuse yourself to any upon earth. Yet you need to do it before heaven and endeavor to expiate your former habitual lewdness with one and cheat on the other by a continued hearty penitence. [Q.2, 9:28, 18 March 1693]

Q. *An impoverished gentleman on whom nature has lavished her stock to render him an unresisted instrument of melting the breasts of the softer sex ... has allured that gift from me which is only due to a husband and would willingly marry me. But my fortune being inconsiderable, I fear I should ... render myself despicable and irretrievably poor.... My friends ... have introduced a gentleman of an inviting estate, ... whose person I could like, had I not first seen my handsome deceiver. I am wracked with confusion what resolution I shall take herein, and since my poor judgment is weak and imperfect, as is common to my sex, I entreat you would speedily impart your friendly advice.*

A. First, repent; then either remain unmarried or marry him that has been so well acquainted with you, for you cannot justly marry any other.... We had not printed this, but that others might take warning by your example. [Q.6, 11:1, 11 July 1693]

Q. *I have long continued in a very vicious course of living, rendering myself incapable of resisting any temptation. First I was guilty of excessive drinking that led to all other mischiefs. It is my misfortune to have contracted too great a familiarity with a woman, who ... endeavors chiefly to seduce me ... and diligently uses all her insinuating charms and deluding stratagems.... Thus, I commit what is afterward the abhorrence of my soul, knowing that while I embrace her in my arms, I only embrace my ruin.... This letter is more important than some questions, ... which encourages me humbly to seek your advice, how I shall disengage myself.*

A. That fornication is damnable without repentance is believed by all but papists and atheists. And as it's plain there's no

repentance without amendment, we expect no amendment while you are near her.... You ought to flee the fair
destroyer, though it was to the ends of the earth. [Q.9, 11:1,
11 July 1693]

Q. *About three years ago, being instigated by the devil and my own
unruly desires, I endeavored to debauch and impose my will on
a certain young woman. But she resisted all my allurements and
countered my designs. Then I rashly wished I might perish if I
ever attempted to do the same again. Notwithstanding that oath,
three months ago (such was the frailty of my nature) I not only
attempted but fully perpetrated that deadly sin, thereby justly mer-
iting that dreadful sentence I had already passed upon myself.
Since the commission of that heinous act, I have had frequent
conflicts within myself about the nature of the same.... Can it be
pardoned? I find myself in a very deplorable condition in respect
to my present state in this world and my future state in the world
to come. Therefore, I heartily beseech you to give me such counsel
and directions as may enable me to make my peace with that God
whom I have so egregiously affronted and may divert his judgment.*

A. Crimes committed after such oaths are almost of the highest nature, since they are in some respect a questioning
of the power and omniscience of God Almighty.... Yet
though such offenses are very heinous our merciful creator
has promised us pardon upon condition of sincere repentance.... Therefore, we should not doubt the goodness and
mercy of God, but watch ourselves carefully so that we
don't give way again to the same temptations. Also, when
any injury is done to another in this as in other cases, some
recompence must be made. That includes endeavors to
convince and if possible reform that person whom we have
seduced. [Q.11, 18:12, 24 August 1695]

Q. *I have been acquainted with a gentleman these six years. He's a single
man and I a single woman, but I can't expect him to marry me*

because his status is above mine. I have kept him company already perhaps beyond the bounds of modesty. I desire to know if I may see him once every three months or more? If not, what method shall I take to avoid seeing him?

A. If you want a dispensation for whoring, you must go to Rome (not to Athens). There you may have it for as many months or as few as you and those soul-jobbers can agree upon it. If you are in earnest when you seem to intimate you would avoid seeing him, there's only one way, which is to retire to some distant place where he may never find you or if he does, be never alone or without the company of some more prudent and virtuous person than yourself. [Q.3, 19:28, 1 February 1696]

Sometimes the sexually active couple pretended they were married when the relationship was discovered, which led to complications.

Q. *A person of good birth and quality has for a long time had . . . a troubled and discontented spirit, which has been caused by his keeping company with a gentlewoman and claiming her amongst his relations and acquaintances for his wife (though they are as yet unmarried). This gentleman tells me he is really contracted to her and thinks in conscience that he ought to marry her, yet he fears it would prove his ruin. She has no fortune and he has already exhausted the greater part of his estate. He has a grandmother and several other relations who depend on him for support. Now, gentlemen, I crave your advice to tell him whether he may with safety abandon this lady and match with another who could repair his estate and so provide for his relations that depend upon him. He is mightily disturbed and has asked my advice. I have taken a week's time to consider. . . . He is resolved to follow my directions, which (to give him ease) must be either to marry or forsake marriage altogether, for I perceive he intends to live a penitent and religious life for the future.*

A. Indeed, sir, it's a little strange that you should take a week's time to consider whether you should advise your friend to be guilty or not guilty of so great a wickedness as habitual adultery as long as he lives, which he must certainly be if he marries any other woman. It is too late now to consider the lady's fortune, for that should have been done before. It's better to retrench his expenses and live a little less well in the world than he would prefer rather than lose his peace and his God. [Q.4, 6:28, 26 March 1692]

Q. *I am an apprentice to an eminent merchant in this city, with whom I have lived almost five years. About a year and a half ago it was my misfortune to fall in love with a young woman born of good parentage, well bred but with no fortune. I have been familiar with her and we have had a child. To save her honor, she told her relatives she was my wife, and indeed I have promised her marriage when my apprenticeship has finished. It has now come to my friends' ears that I am married and I have confessed the whole intrigue to them. Yet they dissuade me from marrying her, which I am much concerned about. Since it is my misfortune, I am resolved to go suddenly into the army, for I am sure that if I should deny that she is my wife, she will destroy herself. I then shall think myself guilty of her death, so I desire your best advice.*

A. If mutual promises passed between you and have been effectually confirmed by the birth of a child, she is undoubtedly your wife before God. According to law you should celebrate the marriage. Your friends seem to place false notions of honor above those of equity and justice. If without your friends' aid you cannot provide for her, you ought in conscience to live unmarried until such time as you can either convince them to help you or no longer need their assistance.... To go to the army would be a very rash resolution, throwing yourself out of your lawful calling, which would make you the less capable of providing for yourself and her that you have made your own. [Q.6, 13:6, 24 February 1694]

Q. *Some time ago it was my misfortune to fall in love with a young woman who lives with her aunt. I never promised her marriage nor did she ever desire marriage, though I received of her all that a woman can give. We went on happily until about two months ago, when our intrigues were discovered by her aunt, who being a religious woman, reproved her. . . . I loved her and did not plan to marry her, yet to save her reputation I told her aunt she was my wife. She believed it and at my request has until now kept it a secret. When I said she was my wife, it was to reinstate her in the favor of the old gentlewoman. I did not intend to speak to her again and so did not visit her for a day or two, but . . . she has now vowed that if ever I cease to visit her, nay cease to love her as I formerly had, she would kill herself. . . . I know that if I visit her, the intrigue will not be a secret for long. . . . Gentlemen, instruct me how to act: if I say she is not my wife, it ruins her; to say she is, ruins me. To keep her company will be trouble and then if I don't see her she vows she will die.*

A. Truly, sir, a fine piece of work! . . . Nothing but a sincere repentance can save you from hellfire. . . . But as for the present emergency, if your generosity will not oblige you to marry that silly wretch to whose debauching and ruin you have been accessory, we see no other obligation for you to marry her if she yielded to you without a promise of marriage. . . . It appears to us much more reasonable for you to abide the calumny and shame of discovery than either to repeat the sin or to make her a more honorable whore by marriage. . . . This is all we can say, hoping it may be a caution to other young persons who have such temptations to be led astray, without considering the shameful and dismal consequence of such a sin. [Q.2, 13:11, 13 March 1694]

Q. *I unhappily became acquainted with one of my own sex, whose manner and person I love and like above all things. She declared the same about me and we vowed a friendship to be kept inviolable until death. But lately I'm assured by undeniable evidence that she has a dishonorable intrigue with a gentleman whom she would have me believe is her husband. I beg your opinion: . . . May I with a good conscience continue our relationship? Or is this a just cause of quitting my friendship, lest I should be one of them . . . who is associated with an adulterer?*

A. We need to be wary of the infectious nature of evil, especially when it insinuates itself under the fair pretense of so amiable a good as friendship. . . . The querist would do very well to break off all correspondence with the criminal person, who by her crimes has first broken this friendship, which can only be between virtuous persons. All this supposes the fact is certain and that the gentleman is really not her husband. [*AO*, 2:96]

Premarital sex could, of course, lead to the birth of illegitimate children. The Athenians answered queries from two women involved in such relationships; the second nominally came from "a friend," but the Athenians assumed the woman herself was the author.

Q. *I have previously troubled you but received no answer. Therefore, I now earnestly entreat you to give your opinion. The past two years and a half I have kept company with a young man by whom I've had two children and am with child again. He always promised me that when his father died, he would recompense me for my favors. My house was also his home. He accepted the use of my purse and table though I did not have much to share with him, for my property is small. At Christmas last, his father died, yet instead of making good his promise, he deserted me and my house. If he can help it, he will not see me. When I ask the reason, he tells me only that he wants to live sober. Pray give me your opinion whether he ought not to compensate me, since he has been the occasion of running me in debt. Or what course should I take?*

A. There's not a word of concern here for your own folly and lewdness.... It's likely enough that there will be thousands of fools after you who will take the same road you have, though they may see their own ruin in yours. For what else can be expected in this world as well as the next, when a helpless woman abandons herself to the lawless desires of any wild rakehell that says he loves her? ... For if even the most sacred bonds of marriage (and so they have been esteemed by all nations) can't restrain some persons and secure their faith to each other, how much less likely is it that a single private promise should be of greater validity, without any such public solemnization?

You must therefore begin a course of severe penitence and mortification for your past lewd and wicked life so you may thereby secure one friend in heaven, though you are now to expect none in this world. You have lost all for which the sex is truly valuable. Then, if your spark continues to treat you as barbarously as he has until now, and if he neither marries you nor provides for you (one of which justice obliges him to do), you must work heartily to maintain yourself and your illegitimate children. That's the best advice we can give you. [Q.4, 16:28, 23 March 1695]

Q. *Reading the first question in this day's* Mercury [Q.1, 18:30, 26 October 1695; see pages 160–61], *you reminded me of a friend of mine, who has delivered up her honor in much the same way.... A man by what charm I know not has now had a son by her. She continues constant to him, even though he rambles the town over, and ... charges her with many faults, which I really believe in my own conscience are untrue. She has had several good offers of marriage but will not accept any, thinking that her sin would be greater if she gave herself to any other man than by continuing with him. I believe that if his old wife dies, he will never marry her. Now I desire your answer whether he is obliged by honor, nay by the laws of God, to marry her considering the contract made between them. They are of an equal age. He has had a child by his wife, who is 30 years older than he is. The other is an agreeable, good-looking woman with wit and a pleasing manner. Therefore, shouldn't he perform all his promises to her? But if he doesn't, may she lawfully marry another?*

A. It's not impossible for the old woman to outlive you both. As he has caused your ruin, he is obliged in gratitude and honor to serve you either by his good advice or interest when he can do it and not injure his family. But if he loves you or himself, he must no longer continue this commerce. We don't think you can succeed with him in any way. Therefore, you ought to quit him wholly and immediately and think of taking care of yourself. First, beg pardon of God Almighty for your offense and absolutely reform. If you can be assured that any of your sparks love you enough to marry you after being acquainted with your circumstances, you can very lawfully accept them. But don't deceive them, and you must be very cautious to whom you entrust such a secret. [Q.4, 19:3, 5 November 1695]

The Athenians responded to a correspondent whom they concluded was trying to reform a wife whose conduct verged on adultery.

Q. *A married lady meets another woman's husband and stays frequently with him in secret some hours at a time. She permits all the freedom and liberty that man and wife are capable of, only the last favor excepted, pretending to act on conscience and principles.... Pray what do you think she means by conscience and principles under such a practice?*

A. Supposing the matter of fact true, it is unnatural hypocrisy and adultery before God.... Whatever little pretenses I have to virtue and honor in outward appearances, if I'm a slave to my lusts and brutish inclinations, the rest avails me nothing. If she could be brought to consider the immediate

sin against God, the injury to the husband, the perjury to
herself in breaking her marriage vows ... and in the end
the afflictions of her real conscience, there might be a way
to reclaim her. We believe it more than probable that this
question was sent by some that wish the lady very well and
would admonish her secretly. We should be glad if it has a
good effect. [Q.4, 9:17, 7 February 1693]

Twice observers of sexual misconduct asked the Athenians for
advice about reporting the behavior.

Q.   *As an apprentice in the city, I discovered my mistress entertained
an unlawful amour with a gentleman who lodged in our house....
The gentleman clapped a guinea into my hand desiring me to
conceal the thing, which I then did. But now I wonder ... am I
bound in conscience to give him his money again and divulge this
matter?*

A.   It would have been convenient to explain whether the
woman were maid, wife, or widow, which would have altered the case. On the whole, ... he ought to advise them if
single to marry or if either is otherwise to cease their criminal conduct. If they refuse, he ought to make it known to
some magistrate. Then they may be punished as the law in
that case provides and bear that infamy which their crimes
deserve. He should return that dishonorable reward which
he received for being a sort of partner in their wickedness
by keeping it concealed from all others. [Q.5, 8:11, 4 October
1692]

Q.   *A very wicked wretch (a neighbor of mine though not of the same
parish) brought up his wife's niece from childhood. He has for
some years past made her his whore and has several children by
her. Query: Does it concern every good Christian (and minister
especially) to take cognizance of such villainy, and do ... all they
can to suppress this complicated sin of incest and adultery? ... I*

humbly beg you to inform me what method is most proper for such
an undertaking.... I am the minister of the next parish.

A. Your method is to refer them all...to the ecclesiastical court.
And the parish may...inquire after support for the children
when there is no visible legal father.... Such members are
a very pernicious scandal to a church and ought to be excommunicated.... We don't look upon the act to be incest.
If you please, you may let us know how you proceed in the
affair and what it comes to. [Q.3, 8:20, 5 November 1692]

Three men sought advice about how to extricate themselves
from adulterous relationships, and a wife asked if she could
enter one to revenge herself upon her unfaithful husband.

Q. *I have long lived in an unlawful though successful amour. I have*
enjoyed all the favors that a lovely young woman can bestow.
I am very sensible of the sin I commit, as well as the injury I do
the husband.... I therefore... beg your advice what measures I shall
take... to avoid the lovely tempter, who will not fail to press me to
a continuance of our passion, which I am resolved to quit.

A. In answer, we first hope the gentleman is in earnest and that
he needs no more arguments to convince him of the absolute necessity there is of his leaving this damnable sin. He
asks what measures he shall take ... to avoid her. But we'll
go further, as we suppose the querist desires, and direct
him how to break off entirely. This we'd advise him not to
do personally... but by letter, in which if he please he may
enclose this paper, which perhaps may make the breach
incurable. If it does, so much the better, for he'll have the
less trouble afterward. [Q.1, 5:13, 12 January 1692]

Q. *I have sworn to continue in an amour with a certain lady.... I*
have promised to live single until it shall please God to take her
husband away and then to marry none but her.... Now I have the
opportunity to marry a virtuous good woman, but am timorous,

*having made such solemn promises to the other lady. Pray please
to give me the best advice.*

A. The whole transaction is very wicked and foolish and such as
God has forbidden. So that if to vow an ill action is a sin, to
continue in the action is a greater one.... Such vows oblige
no persons. All that can be done is to leave the folly and ask
God pardon. Nor is the woman less but rather more to be
blamed than the man, not only for entertaining his amour,
but because God had already settled her condition and provided such a companion for her as he thought convenient.
[Q.3, 5:18, 30 January 1692]

Q. *I'm a young woman ... with an intolerably jealous husband (without provocation, I protest). I lately surprised him with a woman,
and I am now strongly solicited by a gentleman much above my
quality. May I lawfully yield to him those favors not fit to be
mentioned here?*

A. Adultery is absolutely forbidden without any restriction
whatever. God Almighty made no provisions nor other
remedy but a legal divorce.... We know that it is the practice of many to take such a revenge, but ... what an unaccountable folly it is that to ruin myself to vex another....
Your husband injured himself more than you.... Divorce
is the best remedy, provided you have positive proof of his
baseness, although you may perhaps be mistaken as to his
falseness. [Q.1, 8:5, 26 July 1692]

Q. *I have had the misfortune to be very extravagant and wicked and,
among other sins, to be guilty of deluding a married woman. I am
(I hope), through the great goodness of God, become truly sorrowful
for my behavior. I wish to receive Holy Communion but dare not.
Query: May I do it and be a worthy communicant without first
reconciling with the person I have wronged, which I am ready to
do? ... But I do not know any means to effect it without exposing
the woman to her husband and thus cause a rift between them,
which instead of extenuating my sin might add to the enormity.*

A. Since the husband knows nothing of the injury, your revealing it to him by begging his pardon would rather increase the injury, for the knowledge would give him continual disquiets. Since the trespass is of a nature you can never repair or make any satisfaction for, it's much better concealed than revealed.... You are obliged to be silent in your repentance. All you ought to do is to prove your sincerity by a thorough reformation and likewise endeavor to convince the woman you have seduced that she, too, is guilty. [Q.2, 15:14, 20 October 1694]

One man described an adulterous wife who flaunted her infidelity, and two wives had complaints about their husbands having deserted them, one to live with a "whore." The Athenians offered advice to all, but that to the husband was surely more palatable than their recommendations to the women, who were hampered by the near-impossibility of divorce.

Q. *A gentlewoman has a husband who treats her barbarously, placing her in danger of her life. He keeps a whore, refusing to live with his wife, but making her work for her bread. She has the offer of a single gentleman that will maintain her very well. Query: Is it any sin to accept his kindness?*

A. If the words "will maintain" signify "keeping" in the usual sense of it, ... the case is clear. And why all this fine clean language to wrap up that broad word WHORE, with which she so fairly brands one that is kept by her husband, when about to place herself in the same circumstances? Is there any reason why a woman ought to turn whore because her husband is a whoremaster? ... Suppose the gentleman would only generously supply her necessities and expect no criminal returns for his kindness, ... or else rather let's say, pretends to expect none, yet it is ... a dangerous experiment. It is much more honorable and honest to get her living by painful labor, nay almost by begging itself. [Q.2, 5:13, 12 January 1692]

Q.   *I'm a gentlewoman of a small fortune, married to a man who was reported to have a good one, but who I found out had as little as I. He left me with a charge of children and went to another country, without making the least provision either for them or me. Nor will his friends help us. I've been already very chargeable and troublesome to my own friends, who are now grown as cold as his. A gentleman now importunes me very much to be his mistress. I know he loves me passionately and will provide for me and them. I desire your advice what I were best to do, whether I must lay my children to the parish, for begging won't maintain us and stealing is as bad as whoring? Or how ought I to behave myself, for I can find no means but either to yield to this temptation or see my children starve? I know I ought not to do the least evil that good may come of it, but yet of two evils, we must choose the least.*

A.   We do acknowledge it's a sad story and wish it were not true. But we refer to the express words of the commandment: Thou shalt not commit adultery.... If neither her relations nor her husband, knowing of her necessities and temptations, will give her relief, she ought ... to make the parish acquainted with her burden, who by the laws of the land are bound to relieve her.... She and her children ought undoubtedly to beg and suffer the last extremities rather than at the price of her soul avoid them.... It's no sin for her to suffer herself or even to let her children suffer, too, if she has first done all she can to provide for them.... Nay, should she generously and piously refuse any such an unlawful way of supplying her necessities, it's very probable God's providence would find some way to provide an honest subsistence for her and her children, even though none such appear at present. [Q.4, 11:25, 3 October 1693]

Q.   *About three years ago I married a young and handsome woman, and I may say purely out of love, for I was promised but a very inconsiderable estate with her ... yet I loved her entirely. But she like a giddy young creature knew not how to prize the relationship but grew cold in her behavior to me. I was much concerned at my misfortune and used all the endearing ways imaginable to reclaim her ... but she would say ... she would do as she pleased. ... I was then in a good post at sea in the king's service and have been so ever since.*

She would often come on board to see me. By her silly actions there, she made herself odious and me ridiculous. I lost patience and threatened to leave her. ... I had reason enough to suspect her chastity with many, and ... when I promised my pardon she at last confessed it. That was now about a year and a half ago, since which I have had one child by her. ... When I have warned her of her adultery, she maintains her act and vows she does not care if all the world knows it; she seems not in the least sorry for it. ... All my friends have heard of her behavior and I am ashamed to see them. ... Therefore, I have thoughts of leaving her, for ... I can bear it no longer. I am willing to have your advice. ... I am going to sea in a very few days, so pray do not fail to answer ... for I fear a sudden ruin.

Q.1. *Seeing I know her guilty of adultery, notwithstanding I promised her a pardon ... may I lawfully sue out a divorce, having no evidence but her own confession to me?*

Q.2. *May I lawfully leave her to shift for herself if a divorce cannot be had?*

Q.3. *Would it be any sin to marry another woman, she as an adulteress being no wife to me?*

Q.4. *May I lawfully deny her a maintenance, being never content with anything I can do for her?*

Q.5. *If none of this be allowed, how must I carry myself toward her, for to my shame I love her still?*

A. To Q.1. Her justifying so odious a crime is rather worse than her first committing it and makes her ... both uncapable and unworthy of any pardon from God and man. ... You are therefore without doubt at liberty to sue out a divorce,

though her confession to you, if not before a witness, will
not be enough evidence against her. Nor is there any reason
it should be.... You must get substantial witness to the facts
before you can obtain any remedy.

Q.2. Doubtless you may leave her if there's no hope of her
growing better, if you assure her that you'll take this
course if she does not reform.

Q.3. As to remarriage you must be regulated by the laws of
the land, which with good reason make such divorces
very difficult and do not in ordinary circumstances
permit any second marriage. Though the Parliament
could grant it....

Q.4. As for maintaining her, the best part is she'll not know
how to force you to it if you are at sea. We think you
may justly deny it if she continues in her lewd behavior. If she rectifies her errors, you may place funds in
a friend's hand to keep her from want. And the answer to the last query may be easily concluded out of
the former, to which we shall only add, if you are so
unhappy to love her still, discharge her immediately,
keep out of her sight, go away to sea with the next fair
wind, and God send you a bon voyage. [*AO*, 3:205–7]

A wife and a husband each wrote to describe sexual complications caused by in-laws who moved into their household. The
Athenians counseled the wife to involve other relatives as she
sought a solution but advised the husband to keep the matter
confidential to avoid gossip.

Q. *An urgent necessity... causes me to be troublesome to you. My case is
thus: I happened to marry a man whose fortune was much inferior
to mine. After marriage my parents were pleased to get him a gentleman's post. For some time afterward we lived happily together
but then my brother's wife (whose husband died and left her very
well off) came to live with us.... My husband soon became fond of*

*her and withdrew his affection from me. He has ever since treated
me extremely unkindly, and he is now selling our property to turn
it over to her. He wickedly designs to leave me in helpless distress
and ruin. Now pray, gentlemen, . . . I desire you would assist me
with your advice and answer as soon as you can, informing me
what I had best do in this circumstance. You will infinitely oblige
the distressed.*

A. Perhaps he has only threatened you without actually starting
to effect it, and so your kind and courteous behavior may in
time persuade him not to go ahead with his plan. But if you
find he really intends it, inform some of his relations, whose
persuasions and arguments should make him reconsider....
If this still proves unsuccessful, send us the names of the
parties involved, accompanied by proof of the truth of your
story,... and we'll endeavor to publicize both names (if they
both deserve it). [Q.7, 13:20, 14 April 1694]

Q. *Pray tell me what punishment ought to be inflicted upon that man
who attempts to debauch his own brother's wife. After trying al-
luring expressions without success, he endeavored to force her
while swearing a great many execrable oaths. Your speedy answer
is desired, for the wronged brother is ready to pursue immediate
revenge. But he has resolved to take your advice in the matter.
And what should he tell his wife about her behavior in the future,
for she concealed the incident for more than three months before
informing her husband? She explained (and I believe it's true) that
was because he is a very passionate man. They all lived in a house
together with their mother, so that she could not well avoid giving
the brother an occasional opportunity as she was trying to hide so
base an attempt from her husband.*

A. The best revenge is to conquer an enemy by goodness...and
if you can convince your brother of his baseness, reform
him, and make him beg both your pardons; it will be more
honorable than if you stabbed him. But if he continues impenitent, forgive him ... and have no more to do with him

until he is sorry for what he did. If that happens and he convinces you he is sincere, be sure you don't refuse to receive him again as your brother. Any other way of proceeding might only make you the subject of gossip and cannot produce a good effect. As for the lady, if she was no longer in danger perhaps it might not have been amiss if she had never acquainted you with it, knowing your temper. But for the future she only needs to forgive the designed injury and avoid all opportunities of falling into the like misfortunes again. [Q.7, 14:8, 16 June 1694]

The Athenians advised a querist to stop an incestuous marriage in his family, and when a correspondent revealed he suspected similar misbehavior on the part of his beloved, the Athenians declined to speculate. Confronting an admitted case of incest, they counseled silence.

Q.   *Suppose the querist has a daughter about twenty years of age and a brother about the same age, and they happen to have so sincere and earnest a passion for each other that it's feared no reason will prevail to prevent them from marrying. Or, if they are prevented, in all probability that will occasion their ruin in this world. Query: Whether upon this consideration, may the marriage be solemnized with hope of God's blessing and the quiet enjoyment of their liberties and estates to them and their posterity, notwithstanding any scruples that may be raised about it?*

A.   Such a marriage is absolutely unlawful and *ipso facto* void.... We think the gentleman obliged in conscience to hinder this incestuous marriage, whatever the consequences may be. The parties immediately concerned should break off this unlawful amour. [Q.3, 5:13, 12 January 1692]

Q.   *Is a man who has by mistake married his own daughter, coming afterward to know it, obliged to acquaint her with it, if he believes the knowledge of it would occasion her death? And how otherwise ought he to behave himself in that condition, for he has children by her, upon whom the reproach of being so born may bring a great affliction?*

A. He is not assured his revealing it to her will have any such ill effect, but he certainly knows he lives in unlawful embraces, which he is obliged to quit. And why may it not be done with little or no injury to her? ... She is free from guilt because she was ignorant of the offense. They may ... live innocently together as tender friends by parting beds, for which they need not give an account to everyone that may accidentally know it. ... Many handsome pretenses may be made without telling the real cause. This way will also be best for their children, for whose sakes they ought to keep both the world and them ignorant of it. [*AO*, 2:183]

Q. *I have for some time made my application to a lady whom I love beyond expression. She entertains me with ... the strictest rules of virtue and modesty and gives me some assurance of her affection. ... I have several times pressed her to marriage, but she still alleges the extreme love she bears her brother. Her father and mother ... will not permit her to dispose of herself without his consent, which is never likely to be attained, for he is averse to it; and my aversion to him is so great that I could not ... ask him. ... It cannot be for interest she loves him, for he is a clergyman and never likely to leave her anything. Pray, gentlemen, your opinion. ... I am persuaded that the love she bears him must exceed the rules of virtue or else she does not love me at all.*

A. We are unwilling to conclude so uncharitably as you do, though we confess any that reads the story would be tempted to do so. It may be only a just esteem, but we confess that we can't tell what to make of it. [Q.8, 11:1, 11 July 1693]

Both querists and the Athenians worried about sexual gossip. Indeed, on several occasions the Athenians warned male correspondents about their interactions with other men's wives. But in one instance they thought the poor reputation of the gossipers would be enough to clear the name of the injured party.

Q. *Is it permissible to look with pleasure on another woman than one's wife when married or, before marriage, a woman other than one's intended spouse?*

A. It's dangerous, the eye being the burning-glass of love, and looking, liking, desiring, attempting, and criminally obtaining oftentimes or always follow one another. But if it is possible to stop at liking, which is the last step that can be made short of a precipice, we do affirm that is permissible. [Q.4, 1:18, 23 May 1691]

Q. *Is it permissible for a married man to kiss his neighbor's wife out of real respect and affection?*

A. Yes, undoubtedly, ... but it must be an honest affection and respect. Although we may thus love our neighbor's wife, we cannot covet our neighbor's wife. The affection should be pure and innocent, as was that of the primitive Christians in their kiss of peace. [Q.5, 6:7, 23 February 1692]

Q. *Should a man avoid the company and friendship of another's wife (giving no offense to his own wife, nor to her husband), because some people criticize their relationship?*

A. Yes, you ought to refrain. Those that will live unblameably must avoid all appearance of evil, as well as evil itself, for if such involvement is not immediately criminal to yourselves, ... yet since it causes others to sin by spreading scandal and censure, you ought to forbear. Christians ought not to give offenses to one another. [Q.2, 6:26, 26 March 1692]

Q. *Three brothers ... conceived a malice against a near relation because they were disappointed in a lawsuit from which they had hoped to gain a considerable advantage. Hearing she was about to marry a gentleman with a sizeable fortune, they audaciously wrote several letters in their own names, . . . whereby they pretended that one or both had lain with her, which they sent open to one of the brothers. He read it openly at the table at Dick's Coffeehouse between the Temple Gates, boasting of familiarities . . . near 20 years earlier in obscene beastly terms, with purpose to blacken the reputation of the innocent lady and disappoint her marriage. These three brothers are notoriously known as scandalous libertines and known defamers of the reputations of those they could never debauch. Being conscious they had run themselves into the danger of the law, they flew into the country to shelter themselves.*

Gentlemen, your sage advice and sense of this matter is desired with all speed. Will you prescribe her the means to punish so egregious a baseness? . . . How shall innocence pretend to guard itself from the lash of such backbiting tongues and the poisonous rancor of such malicious contrivances and combinations?

A. We suppose publishing the relation is of more consequence to the lady than any answer to it, for we take it for granted that if she were guilty she would never desire the world should know it. . . . We think there's no need of any guard of that innocence mentioned in the question, since the aggressors by their absconding acknowledge themselves guilty and clear the calumny. [Q.3, 9:17, 7 February 1693]

Q. *A gentleman has a great friendship for a young lady and she no less for him. That brings them frequently together without giving any offense to her husband or his wife. The gentleman desires to know whether they are obliged to stop seeing each other because some people surmise that their frequent meetings are not innocent and discourse about them?*

A. The world is so wicked that some may be censorious. For that reason, wise people will be very cautious, because if possible it's a duty to avoid causeless offenses. If you know yourselves to be innocent you are so much the happier, but you must likewise do something on account of others.

Therefore, you should avoid such meetings as will make persons talk, but if you meet in the company of others, we don't think that anything injurious can occur. [Q.1, 16:19, 19 February 1695]

Q. *I have a very intimate acquaintance whose wife is very kind and familiar with me. If I don't kiss her, she'll kiss me and take other greater familiarities. Her infirm husband seems well pleased with our relationship. I'm a single man and would not be rude to her. Pray tell me whether such interactions be permissible, provided I proceed no further.*

A. The truth is that your friend's wife is very friendly and familiar with you, but whether innocently so is not clear in this world. But there is one in the other that knows you better than you do yourself, and you know what he says about men who deal another's wife in such a way. Even though such practices are not directly criminal, their consequences are so dangerous that you ought to change your actions if you value your own honor or happiness. [Q.5, 17:7, 23 April 1695]

Three correspondents asked about possibly pursuing a second marriage with a potential spouse they already knew. The second question below obliquely revealed premarital sex with the first husband.

Q. *It is my misfortune to fix my affections on . . . another's wife, which has made me often endeavor to stifle my passion, but in vain. . . . Queries: May the lady within the rules of modesty, and with a due respect to her own virtue and honor, make me a conditional promise if she should survive her husband, without breaking the vow she made him in marriage? And is such a request from me a breach of the Tenth Commandment, because it would only be effective after the death of her husband?*

A. The relation is a very great folly and wickedness. It is a folly to wait for anything . . . since our lover does not know

whether he or his mistress may one or both die before the
husband.... If she agrees to such a conditional promise,
it necessarily follows ... that it will alienate her affections
from her lawful husband and then there's a gate open to
many horrid practices.... Such a person must certainly be
in a state of damnation. Therefore, our advice is that he repent himself of such a wicked folly and prove the sincerity
of his repentance by avoiding all opportunities to see her,
which may renew so vile a flame. [Q.6, 6:25, 26 March 1692]

Q. *Two gentlemen courted me, one very well accomplished, the other
rough and unpolished. Both passionately loved me. I loved, liked,
and admired the genteel spark, but the other would take no denial, so I was compelled to marry him. Considering a speedy
marriage was necessary, I yet retain some kindness for my former
admirer. I beg to know whether such sentiments be absolutely
criminal, and if fate ever allow me my freedom, may I have him
for my second husband, who but for some fatal circumstances
had been my first?*

A. It is sin and folly to entertain any other thoughts than what a
virtuous friendship will admit and perhaps that is not safe
neither.... A quiet and peaceable mind is preferable to all
enjoyments whatever, and that's never to be got except by
those who endeavor to be content with their condition.
[Q.4, 11:5, 25 July 1693]

Q. *My wife was prudent, wise, and virtuous, her mind and person agreeable. But she had a virtuous friend and companion, perfectly well
accomplished, with all the good qualifications of her sex.... Unknown to her and against my own reason I felt affection for her that
was more properly due to my wife. This incomparable woman no
sooner recognized my inclination for her but she left us and went
into a far country to avoid damage to her and my reputations. This
honorable as well as innocent retreat almost broke my heart.... I
did swear, vow, and faithfully promise before and in the presence*

of God Almighty to take her to be my second wife if ever the first
would be taken from me.... And now my wife, to the great grief
of both of us, is dead and I am free from any obligation.... This
lady does not dissuade me from fulfilling my vow, but my family,
children, and business concerns forbid me to marry her, and bid
me marry another woman.

Q.1. *Am I obliged to perform my vow in favor of her, who is the*
best woman alive, or should I obey the dictates of my friends,
children, family necessities, and other affairs, and marry
another woman?

Q.2. *What power had I to make such a promise while my other*
wife was living?

A.1. Poor man, your case is deplorable, being overcome with
the mighty grief and affliction for the loss of such a good
wife ... but it seems she being gone, you find it expedient
to noose again.... We'll give our consent, but advise you ...
not to marry your incomparable lady, for being once your
own she'll soon lose all her merit and become the same
dull, insipid thing as your former wife.... If she's as wise
as you report her to be, she'll not easily venture on a man
who could violate his duty to his first wife.... Besides, in
this matter you must pay attention to your own affairs, and
neither ruin her, yourself, or children.

A.2. Such promises are foolish because a person is not certain
he shall be in a capacity to perform them.... Yet once made
we believe them obligatory and they can only become void
by a mutual consent.... You ought to remain as you are until
either your affairs will agree with your love or your love give
way to your affairs. [Q.1, 18:5, 30 July 1695]

Two especially scandalous tales bring this book to an end. One
story, indeed, was so scandalous the Athenians suspected it
was fictional, drawn from a contemporary novel. Once again
the Athenians displayed their dry wit in responses to both
questions.

Q. *Five years ago I married a gentlewoman only for her virtue and beauty, which she yet retains to the highest degree. A friend to us both ... tells me he is passionately in love with my wife and without enjoyment of her shall lay violent hands on himself. ... Considering he is my friend, I ought to assist him, but considering she is my wife I ought not. ... She purely to oblige me has agreed, though reluctantly, and desires it may be deferred till we have your opinion. Is it a sin for one or all three of us; and if a sin, is it not better to commit it, than for our good friend to kill himself? The former may be repented, but the latter, according to the Bible, must be his inevitable damnation.*

A. If ever a story had the air of a romance, this certainly does (and indeed there's a novel extant much like it). But if it be really true, sure they are all three raving mad, for that's the most charitable opinion we can have on the matter. ... But supposing the spark in any haste or necessity of killing himself, which it seems he is not, for he can wait until he hears our answer, better he should do so than that all three be guilty of willfully planned adultery, a damning sin. [Q.7, 6:7, 23 February 1692]

Q. *A well-bred gentleman friend of mine, who lost his fortune by cross fate, had the misfortune to meet two gentlewomen, one of them married but childless. She had a great desire to enjoy the blessing of children and proposed to bestow her favors on the aforesaid gentleman, who was so much charmed by her intrigues that he could not avoid being deluded by her. She, wishing to enjoy his constant presence, further ensnared him by persuading him after only four days' acquaintance to marry the other gentlewoman, who was her cousin. They got him before an excommunicated parson when he was drunk and there they were married. They lived together fourteen days, but then some ill-tempered people, especially her friends, were not pleased with their marriage. They spread a most scandalous aspersion about the gentleman, which the woman believed and left him. ... He has often written to her for a year and a half, but he has not heard from her, except to learn that she will not own him as her husband, although his person and virtues deserve a better wife.*

   Query: Now he desires to know how he shall behave himself in this matter and if the marriage is lawful. Should he discharge his duty by compelling her to live and die with him? Although she has no fortune, he does mightily repent his folly with the married woman and indeed with either, for it has hindered his preferment. Your opinion and advice are earnestly desired.

A. Your friend has made the proverb good with a vengeance—marry in haste, repent at leisure—and he must take its due reward, repentance, for his pains. Although a person that acts so palpably contrary to reason hardly deserves any pity, yet…we shall give him our advice and good wishes.… Although a minister under excommunication ought not to perform any such part of his function, after it is done it is of force. It is very plain that both people consented and probable that nothing essential to matrimony was lacking.… She is lawfully his wife and if he can maintain her, he may and would do well to oblige her to live with him. [Q.4, 12:19, 26 December 1693]

CODA

THE *MERCURY* APPEARED BETWEEN 17 March 1691 and 17 June 1697; by the end of its run, interest in the queries had fallen off and the content had changed its focus to include more essays and poetry, especially by female authors. After the *Mercury* ceased publication, all three collaborators encountered financial difficulties. Richard Sault moved to Cambridge, where he continued his work as a teacher of mathematics until he fell seriously ill and died in 1702. By then, his wife had accused him of philandering, a charge he publicly admitted was true. Samuel Wesley became the rector of Epworth, Lincolnshire, where he spent the rest of his life as a clergyman and author until his death in 1735. Constantly in debt, he frequently involved himself in political and religious controversies. He and his wife, Susanna, despite a fractious relationship, had seventeen children, among them John and Charles Wesley, the founders of Methodism.

John Dunton never recaptured the success of the *Mercury*, although he tried, continuing his career as a prolific printer and author. Along with his own declining health, his grief over his first wife Elizabeth's death in May 1697 seemingly contributed to his decision to stop publishing the broadsheet. But then he adopted a course of action the Athenians had advised against—quickly remarrying for money later that same year. When his second wife's wealthy widowed mother understood his motive, she refused to finance him further, and he and his new wife soon separated. Desperate for funds, he sold the copyrights to the *Mercury*; the new owner, Andrew Bell, edited and reprinted many of the questions and answers in three, later four, volumes

Memorandum

67

That it is agreed between John
Dunton Citizen and Stationer of
London, on the one part and Andrew
Bell of the same That y[e] s[d] Jn[o] Dunton
shall sell to y[e] s[d] Andr: Bell, a Copy
Intitled y[e] Athenian Oracle &c, which
shall Contain in Print of a large Octavo —
Long Primer, betwixt thirty or forty Sheets
as to y[e] s[d] Andr Bell shall seeme most
Convenient: For each sheet thereof y[e] s[d]
Andr Bell shall Pay to y[e] s[d] John Dunton
Ten Shillings P[r] sheet, at y[e] finishing or Print-
ing of each six sheets, That it be Put to three
Printing Houses That it may be finished if
possible by y[e] first of January next, and
that Mr Grantham be one of y[e] Printers, provided
his Letter be such as y[e] s[d] Andr Bell approves on
and that he will do it as cheap as another. —
And that y[e] s[d] Andr Bell do Oblidge each
Printer to let George Larkin sen[r] have y[e] Correcting of each sheet of y[e] s[d] Book, & to be paid
for it by them at y[e] rate it is usually P[d] to other
Correctors, That y[e] s[d] Andr Bell do give to y[e] s[d]
Jn[o] Dunton twelve Books B[d] in calves leather
as soon as they are Published, That if y[e] s[d] Andr Bell
shall think fit to go on wth a Second, third or fourth
Vol[m] each Vol shall be on y[e] same terms: and if
the s[d] Andr Bell shall think fit Not to go on wth not to
go on wth another Vol, that it shall be lawfull for y[e] s[d]
Jn[o] Dunton in whom y[e] Propriety of y[e] s[d] Copy is, to go on w[th]
y[e] s[d] Copy himself, or dispose of it to any other, after
the s[d] Andr Bell has refused it, In confirmation
of w[ch] s[d] Articles y[e] s[d] Andr Bell has given a Guinea to
for y[e] use of y[e] Proprietor of y[e] fifteen vol of y[e]
Athenian Mercuries B[d] up together, in full & has also
Hereunto Subscribed his name this Seventh Day of
Novembr. 1702   Andrew Bell

Witness
George Larkin

FIGURE 8. Contract between John Dunton and Andrew Bell for *The Athenian Oracle*, 7 November 1702. The Bodleian Libraries, University of Oxford, MS. Rawl. D72, fol. 121r.

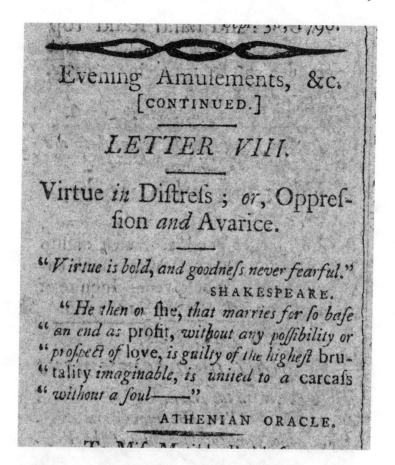

FIGURE 9. On 15 September 1796, the Portsmouth, New Hampshire, newspaper *Oracle of the Day* reprinted a brief excerpt from one of *The Athenian Oracle*'s comments on love and marriage, then approximately a century old but obviously still regarded as relevant. Courtesy of the American Antiquarian Society.

titled *The Athenian Oracle*, which appeared between 1703 and 1711. That collection remained of enduring interest throughout the eighteenth century; it was read in the American colonies at least as late as the 1790s, and occasional references to it appeared in American newspapers throughout the nineteenth century.

ATHENIANISM was John Dunton's thought.
And in these features to Perfection brought:
For Knight and Gucht that Mystick Art did find,
To paint John's PROJECTS person, and his Mind.
They with the likeness, warmth and Grace do give,
And make his Picture seem to think and live:
And's Heraldry he from the Muses farms,
For PEGASUS shou'd be a Poets Arms.

FIGURE 10. This portrait of John Dunton, by J. B. Nichols, is the frontispiece in Dunton's autobiography, *The Life and Errors of John Dunton* (London, 1705). Reproduced by permission from the Huntington Library, San Marino, California.

In later years Dunton continued to struggle financially despite producing publications until 1728. The most important was his autobiography, *The Life and Errors of John Dunton, Citizen of London* (1705), one of the first autobiographies written in English. But like his other works—authored, edited, or printed—it failed to attract many purchasers. At intervals he endured imprisonment for debt and, without children, relied heavily on the charity of friends before his death in 1732.

In early 1801, the editor of a Philadelphia newspaper, the *Repository and Weekly Register*, borrowed a copy of *The Athenian Oracle* from a friend. Over the next few months, he reprinted a few excerpts. He asked if any of his readers could supply "an account of the society, with whom it originated." No one seems to have answered.

FURTHER READING

Berry, Helen. *Gender, Society, and Print Culture in Late Stuart England: The Cultural World of the* Athenian Mercury. Burlington, VT: Ashgate, 2003.

Brewer, Holly. *By Birth or Consent: Children, Law, and the Anglo-American Revolution in Authority*. Chapel Hill: University of North Carolina Press, 2005.

Cowan, Brian. "What Was Masculine about the Public Sphere? Gender and the Coffeehouse Milieu in Post-Restoration England." *History Workshop Journal* 51 (Spring 2001): 127–57.

Dunton, John. *The Life and Errors of John Dunton Late Citizen of London*... London: S. Malthus, 1705.

Gowing, Laura. *Domestic Dangers: Women, Words, and Sex in Early Modern London*. Oxford: Clarendon Press, 1996.

———. *Women's Worlds in Seventeenth-Century England*. New York: Routledge, 2000.

Hunt, Margaret. *The Middling Sort: Commerce, Gender, and the Family in England, 1680–1780*. Berkeley: University of California Press, 1996.

Laqueur, Thomas. *Making Sex: Body and Gender from the Greeks to Freud*. Cambridge, MA: Harvard University Press, 1990.

McDowell, Paula. *The Women of Grub Street: Press, Politics, and Gender in the London Literary Marketplace, 1678–1730*. Oxford: Clarendon Press, 1998.

McEwen, Gilbert. *The Oracle of the Coffee House: John Dunton's* Athenian Mercury. San Marino, CA: Huntington Library, 1972.

Norton, Mary Beth. *Founding Mothers & Fathers: Gendered Power and the Forming of American Society*. New York: Alfred A. Knopf, 1996.

———. *Separated by Their Sex: Women in Public and Private in the Colonial Atlantic World*, especially chapter 3. Ithaca, NY: Cornell University Press, 2011.

Parks, Stephen. *John Dunton and the English Book Trade*. New York: Garland, 1976.

Pincus, Steve. "'Coffee Politicians Does Create': Coffeehouses and Restoration Political Culture." *Journal of Modern History* 67 (1995): 807–34.

Shepard, Alexandra. *Meanings of Manhood in Early Modern England*. New York: Oxford University Press, 2003.

Shevelow, Kathryn. *Women and Print Culture: The Construction of Femininity in the Early Periodical*. London: Routledge, 1989.

Stone, Lawrence. *The Family, Sex and Marriage in England, 1500–1800*. London: Penguin, 1977.

Tadmor, Naomi. *Family and Friends in Eighteenth-Century England: Household, Kinship, and Patronage*. New York: Cambridge University Press, 2001.

INDEX

NOTE: Page numbers in *italic* type indicate illustrations.

procreation. *See* sexual reproduction/
procreation
promises, 88–110; behavior amount-
ing to, 92; breaking of pieces of
money to signal, 82, 88, 90, 102,
160; broken, 35, 63–64, 89–90, 94;
death as factor in keeping/mak-
ing, 99, 103, 113, 125, 148, 184–86;
under false pretenses or coercion,
96–97, 107; marriage ceremony
contrasted with private, 7, 11, 89,
98, 113–19, 134–35, 166–69; mutual
consent to abandon, 88–90;
obligation to keep, 36, 42–44,
57, 63–64, 76, 79, 81–84, 88–110;
parental consent in opposition to
child's, 70–71, 74–75; seriousness
of, 93–94; sexual misbehavior
as reason for voiding, 108–9; for
wrongdoing not considered valid,
155. *See also* vows, marriage
property/estate: bequeathing of, 53;
husbands' behavior concerning,
130; marriage vows and, 62; wives'
behavior concerning, 129–32.
See also finances; social status
prostitution, 7, 117. *See also* whores and
whoring

querists. *See* correspondents

red hair, 28
reform. *See* repentance/penitence/
mortification/reformation
Reformation of Manners, 7
rejection of affection/love: despair
over, 26–27; fear of, 22, 25; healthy
responses to, 22, 27; proper behavior of the agent in, 27; responsibility for consequences of, 34–36
relatives. *See* friends; parental consent
for marriage; parents; siblings
religion: as a consideration in
marriage, 52, 64; differences in,
124–25; parental obligations and,
86–87. *See also* laws of God; Ten
Commandments

repentance/penitence/mortification/
reformation, 34, 44, 109, 116, 128,
143, 151, 152, 163–66, 168, 170, 171,
175, 178, 179–80, 185, 188. *See also*
pardon seeking
Repository and Weekly Register (newspaper), 193
reproduction. *See* sexual
reproduction/procreation
reputation: of a man, 70, 76, 85, 148;
of a woman, 46–47, 129, 140, 161,
168, 183
respect, 24, 32, 36, 56, 62, 87, 132, 134,
158, 182, 184
responsibility. *See* morality
rivals: advice sought concerning,
37–42; divulging of information
about, 38–40; opportunities for,
18, 19

sacrament. *See* communion
sailors, 23, 34–35, 102, 112, 148, 177–78
same-sex relationships, 96, 151–52,
154, 168–69
Sault, Richard, 2, 5, 7, 189
Savior, 129, 159
second marriages: parental consent
not needed for, 86–87; planning
for, in event of a spouse's death,
184–86; prohibited after divorce,
138, 149–50, 178
secrets and secrecy: divulging of,
in cases of misconduct, 38–40,
69–70, 172–73; divulging of, to a
lover, 109, 158. *See also* marriage:
public vs. private
separation, marital, 138, 140–41
servants: marriage to, 114; masters'
impregnation of, 115, 127–29, 157;
as status symbol, 29
sexual relations: absence of, in
marriage, 136, 147–49; absten-
tion from, 135–37; gossip about,
181–84; obligation to divulge,
172–73; promises voided because
of, 108–9; role of, in definition
of marriage, 113–19, 122, 148,

162; urges for, 147–48 (*see also* masturbation). *See also* adultery; consummation of marriage; cuckoldry; extramarital sex; fornication; prostitution; temptation; whores and whoring
sexual reproduction/procreation: financial hardships brought on by, 135–37; means of preventing, 136–37; obstacles to, 29; as purpose of marriage, 53, 136
siblings: and adulterous behavior, 179–80; incest between, 181; intervention of, in courtship, 30, 57–58. *See also* friends
sin: extramarital sex, 31, 115–18, 165, 170–72; marital obligations, 103, 125, 127–28, 147; marriage without parental consent, 74, 79; masturbation, 154–55; swearing falsely, 162–63. *See also* adultery; laws of God; repentance/penitence/mortification/reformation; temptation; Ten Commandments
slighting: advice sought in cases of, 12, 17; contemptuous nature of, 32; proper use of, 27, 96, 139; responsibility for consequences of, 35–36
social status: Athenians' attitude toward, 13; of correspondents, 10, 64; in courtship, 29–30, 96. *See also* finances; property/estate
sparks (beaus), 14, 23, 76–78, 91, 104, 105, 158, 160, 170, 185, 187
Stuart monarchy, 5–6

temptation, guarding against, 31, 65–66, 138, 147–48, 152–55
Ten Commandments, 122, 125, 154, 176, 184
tobacco, 29, 136

virginity, 46, 56, 155–56
virtue. *See* character; honor
vows, marriage, 62–65, 96. *See also* promises

Ward, Edward, *Vulgus Britannicus: or the British Hudibras*, 8
Wesley, Charles, 189
Wesley, John, 189
Wesley, Samuel, 2, 5, 7, 189
Wesley, Susanna, 189
whores and whoring, 34, 55, 128, 138, 139, 146, 166, 168, 172, 175, 176. *See also* adultery; extramarital sex; prostitution
widows, 52, 56, 123–24
William of Orange, 5–6
wit/intelligence, 26, 45, 55–56, 59–61, 81, 86, 91, 109, 120, 134, 155, 171
wives: advice for abused, 138; advice sought for finding, 21; behavior of, before and after marriage, 122; complain of husbands' behavior, 137–39, 141–43; husbands' complaints about behavior of, 137–42; marital role of, 11; selection of, 52, 56–57, 60–61
women: Athenians' attitude toward, 12–13; as coffeehouse workers, 6, 8; courtship behavior of, 18, 47–49; friendships with men, 37–38, 45–47, 182–85; friendships with women, 168–69; honor of, 31–32, 34–35, 49, 163, 167; love between, 151–52; marital behavior of, 53; marriage outcomes for, 120; modesty of, 17, 21–23, 48, 145–46, 181, 184; reputation of, 46–47, 129, 140, 161, 168, 183; as street vendors of the *Athenian Mercury*, 4, 5. *See also* letters from women; wives